Federal Reserve: Emergency Lending

Updated March 27, 2020

Congressional Research Service

https://crsreports.congress.gov

R44185

Summary

The 2007-2009 financial crisis led the Federal Reserve (Fed) to revive an obscure provision found in Section 13(3) of the Federal Reserve Act (12 U.S.C. 344) to extend credit to nonbank financial firms for the first time since the 1930s. Section 13(3) provides the Fed with greater flexibility than its normal lending authority. Using this authority, the Fed created six broadly based facilities (of which only five were used) to provide liquidity to "primary dealers" (certain large investment firms) and to revive demand for commercial paper and asset-backed securities. More controversially, the Fed provided special, tailored assistance exclusively to four firms that the Fed considered "too big to fail"—AIG, Bear Stearns, Citigroup, and Bank of America.

In response to the financial turmoil caused by the coronavirus disease 2019 (COVID-19), the Fed reopened four of these broadly-based programs and created two new ones in 2020. Treasury pledged $50 billion of assets from the Exchange Stabilization Fund (ESF) to protect the Fed against losses in most of these programs. H.R. 748, referred to by some as the "third coronavirus stimulus" bill, was passed by the Senate on March 25, 2020. The bill would provide between $454 billion and $500 billion to support Fed liquidity facilities. The bill states that applicable requirements of Section 13(3) shall apply to these facilities.

Credit outstanding (extended in the form of cash or securities) authorized by Section 13(3) peaked at $710 billion in November 2008. All credit extended under Section 13(3) during the financial crisis was repaid with interest. Contrary to popular belief, the Fed earned profits of more than $30 billion and did not suffer any losses on transactions authorized by Section 13(3). These transactions exposed the taxpayer to greater risks than traditional discount window lending to banks, however, because in some cases the terms of the programs had fewer safeguards.

The Fed's use of Section 13(3) in the 2007-2009 crisis raised fundamental policy issues: Should the Fed be lender of last resort to banks only, or to all parts of the financial system? Should the Fed lend to firms that it does not supervise? How much discretion does the Fed need to be able respond to unpredictable financial crises? How can Congress ensure that taxpayers are not exposed to losses? Do the benefits of emergency lending outweigh the costs, including moral hazard? How can Congress ensure that Section 13(3) is not used to "bail out" failing firms? Should the Fed tell Congress and the public to whom it has lent?

The restrictions in Section 13(3) placed few limits on the Fed's actions in 2008. However, in 2010, the Dodd-Frank Wall Street Reform and Consumer Protection Act (P.L. 111-203) added more restrictions to Section 13(3), attempting to ban future assistance to failing firms while maintaining the Fed's ability to create broadly based facilities. The Dodd-Frank Act also required records for actions taken under Section 13(3) to be publicly released with a lag and required the Government Accountability Office (GAO) to audit those programs. Although Section 13(3) must be used "for the purpose of providing liquidity to the financial system," some Members of Congress have expressed interest in—while others have expressed opposition to—the Fed using Section 13(3) to assist financially struggling entities, including states, municipalities, and territories of the United States.

Jeb Hensarling, former Chairman of the House Financial Services Committee, contends that "Dodd-Frank tried but failed to rein in the Fed's emergency lending authority." Legislation was passed by the House in the 114th Congress (H.R. 3189) and 115th Congress (H.R. 10) that would have further limited the Fed's authority under Section 13(3). Then-Federal Reserve Chair Janet Yellen contended that such restrictions would "essentially repeal the Federal Reserve's remaining ability to act in a crisis." Current Fed Chairman Jerome Powell opposed further reducing the

Fed's discretion under Section 13(3) on the grounds that the Fed needs "to be able to respond flexibly and nimbly" to threats to financial stability.

Contents

Figures

Tables

Appendixes

Contacts

Introduction

The financial crisis that began in 2007 and deepened in 2008 was the worst since the Great Depression. The federal policy response was swift, large, creative, and controversial, creating unprecedented tools to grapple with financial instability. Particularly notable were the actions taken by the Federal Reserve (Fed) under its broad emergency lending authority, Section 13(3) of the Federal Reserve Act (12 U.S.C. 344). This obscure section of the act was described in a 2002 review as follows: "To some this lending legacy is likely a harmless anachronism, to others it's still a useful insurance policy, and to others it's a ticking time bomb of political chicanery."[1]

Using its normal powers, the Fed faces statutory limitations on whom it may lend to, what it may accept as collateral, and for how long it may lend. Because many of the actions it took during the crisis did not meet these limitations, Section 13(3) was used to authorize most of the Fed's emergency facilities created during the crisis to provide credit to nonbank financial firms. More controversially, the Fed also invoked Section 13(3) to prevent the failure of—some would say to "bail out"—Bear Stearns and American International Group (AIG), two financial firms that it deemed "too big to fail." The Federal Reserve also lent extensively to banks through the discount window and newly created facilities and undertook "quantitative easing" (large scale purchases of Treasury and mortgage-backed securities) during the crisis.[2] Because these actions were taken under other authorities, they are beyond the scope of this report, as are other actions taken by the federal government during the crisis.[3]

The Dodd-Frank Wall Street Reform and Consumer Protection Act (hereinafter, the Dodd-Frank Act; P.L. 111-203) limited the Fed's discretion under Section 13(3), but some Members of Congress believe that these changes were insufficient.

In response to the financial turmoil caused by the coronavirus disease 2019 (COVID-19), the Fed reopened some of these programs in 2020. It has also taken other actions to promote economic activity and financial stability that are not taken under Section 13(3). For an overview of these actions, see CRS Insight IN11259, *Federal Reserve: Recent Actions in Response to COVID-19*, by Marc Labonte. H.R. 748, referred to by some as the "third coronavirus stimulus" bill, was passed by the Senate on March 25, 2020. The bill would provide between $454 billion and $500 billion to support Fed liquidity facilities. (Of the $500 billion, $46 billion could be used to support specifically identified industries. Any sum that is not spent from this $46 billion could be used to support Fed facilities.) The bill states that applicable requirements of Section 13(3) shall apply to these facilities.

This report provides a review of the history of Section 13(3), including its use in 2008 and 2020. It discusses the Fed's authority under Section 13(3) before and after the Dodd-Frank Act. It then discusses policy issues and previous legislation to amend Section 13(3), including H.R. 3189, which passed the House on November 19, 2015.

---

[1] David Fettig, *Lender of More than Last Resort*, Federal Reserve Bank of Minneapolis, December 1, 2002, at https://www.minneapolisfed.org/publications/the-region/lender-of-more-than-last-resort.

[2] For more information, see CRS Report RL30354, *Monetary Policy and the Federal Reserve: Current Policy and Conditions*, by Marc Labonte.

[3] For an overview, see CRS Report R43413, *Costs of Government Interventions in Response to the Financial Crisis: A Retrospective*, by Baird Webel and Marc Labonte.

History of Section 13(3)

One of the main reasons the Fed was created was to act as a "lender of last resort," by providing liquidity in the form of short-term loans to banks through the discount window. The Fed still provides that service today, but the amount of liquidity extended is insignificant typically. Over time, it became expected that banks would meet their short-term borrowing needs through private markets under normal conditions. Discount window lending to banks occurs under the Fed's normal statutory authority.

Nonbank financial firms also face liquidity needs, but the history of Fed lending to nonbanks is much more limited. Section 13(3) has been invoked rarely since it was enacted in 1932. The Fed used it to make 123 loans to nonfinancial firms totaling $1.5 million from 1932 to 1936, until that authority was superseded by new authority (Section 13b, which was subsequently repealed).[4] Section 13(3) can also be used to authorize lending to banks. After 1936, the Fed invoked Section 13(3) occasionally to make nonmember banks and credit unions eligible to borrow at the discount window before 1980, when nonmember banks were permitted to access the discount window.[5] Section 13(3) authority was not used to extend credit to nonbanks from 1936 to 2008. This authority was then used extensively beginning in 2008 in response to the financial crisis—in very different ways than it had been used previously.

Use of Section 13(3) in 2020 in Response to COVID-19

In March 2020, the Fed opened six lending facilities using Section 13(3) authority in response to financial disruptions caused by COVID-19 in markets for corporate debt, municipal debt, and nonresidential asset-backed securities:

- **Commercial Paper Funding Facility (CPFF).** The Fed revived the CPFF, which uses a special purpose vehicle (SPV)[6] created and controlled by the Fed to support the *commercial paper market*.[7] Commercial paper is short-term debt issued by financial firms (including banks), nonfinancial firms, and pass-through entities that issue asset-backed securities (ABS). The CPFF purchases newly-issued commercial paper from all types of U.S. issuers who cannot find private sector buyers. Issuers must pay a fee to the Fed, as well as interest on the commercial paper; the interest rate is set at the prevailing three-month overnight index swap rate plus two percentage points. There are limits on how much

---

[4] Howard Hackley, *Lending Functions of the Federal Reserve Banks*, Federal Reserve, 1973, p. 130. See also David Fettig, *Lender of More than Last Resort*, Federal Reserve Bank of Minneapolis, December 1, 2002, at https://www.minneapolisfed.org/publications/the-region/lender-of-more-than-last-resort; James Dolley, "The Industrial Advance Program of the Federal Reserve System," *The Quarterly Journal of Economics*, vol. 50, no. 2, February 1936, p. 229.

[5] Nationally chartered banks are required to be members of the Federal Reserve System. State chartered banks have the option of becoming members. Until the Monetary Control Act of 1980 (P.L. 96-221), only member banks were allowed to borrow at the discount window.

[6] The Fed's use of SPVs is discussed in more detail below in the section entitled "Lending to Itself?"

[7] Federal Reserve, "Federal Reserve Board Announces Establishment Of A Commercial Paper Funding Facility (CPFF) To Support The Flow Of Credit To Households And Businesses," press release, March 17, 2020, at https://www.federalreserve.gov/newsevents/pressreleases/monetary20200317a.htm.

commercial paper any issuer can sell to the facility, and the commercial paper must receive a relatively high credit rating to be eligible for purchase. The CPFF is currently scheduled to expire in March 2021. Treasury has pledged $10 billion of assets from the Exchange Stabilization Fund to protect the Fed from future losses.

- **Primary Dealer Credit Facility (PDCF).** The Fed revived the PDCF to provide liquidity to primary dealers,[8] a group of large government securities dealers that are market makers in securities markets and are the Fed's traditional counterparties for open market operations.[9] The PDCF can be thought of as analogous to a discount window for primary dealers. Loans are made at the Fed's primary credit rate (i.e., the borrowing rate at the discount window), which is currently set at the top of the federal funds target range. Loans are available with maturities ranging from overnight to up to 90 days, with recourse (i.e., loans must still be repaid if collateral is insufficient); and they are fully collateralized, limiting their riskiness. Acceptable collateral includes U.S. Treasuries; government agency debt; investment grade corporate, mortgage-backed, asset-backed, and municipal securities; and certain classes of equities.

- **Money Market Fund Liquidity Facility (MMLF).** The Fed created the MMLF to make nonrecourse loans to financial institutions to purchase assets that money market funds are selling to meet redemptions.[10] This reduces the probability of runs on money market funds caused by a fund's inability to liquidate assets. Only assets sold by prime money market funds or funds that invest in municipal debt are eligible for the MMLF. Securities eligible for purchase include U.S. Treasuries; securities issued by government agencies or government-sponsored enterprises; highly rated municipal debt that matures in less than 12 months; and highly rated commercial paper. The Fed earns interest on the loans (at the prime credit rate for Treasury, government agency, or government sponsored debt, plus an additional 0.25 percentage points for municipal debt, and an additional one percentage point for commercial paper) but bears the risk that the security will decline below the value of the loan. On March 19, 2020, the banking regulators issued an interim final rule so that these loans would not affect the borrowing bank's compliance with regulatory capital requirements.[11]

- **Primary Market Corporate Credit Facility (PMCCF) and Secondary Market Corporate Credit Facility (SMCCF).** The Fed created two new facilities to support corporate bond markets—the PMCCF to purchase newly issued corporate debt from issuers and the SMCCF to purchase existing corporate

---

[8] For a list of current primary dealers and more information about their relationship with the Fed, see https://www.newyorkfed.org/markets/primarydealers.

[9] Federal Reserve, "Federal Reserve Board Announces Establishment Of A Primary Dealer Credit Facility (PDCF) To Support The Credit Needs Of Households And Businesses," press release, March 17, 2020, at https://www.federalreserve.gov/newsevents/pressreleases/monetary20200317b.htm.

[10] Federal Reserve, "Federal Reserve Board broadens program of support for the flow of credit to households and businesses by establishing a Money Market Mutual Fund Liquidity Facility (MMLF)," press release, March 18, 2020, at https://www.federalreserve.gov/newsevents/pressreleases/monetary20200318a.htm.

[11] Federal Reserve, Federal Deposit Insurance Corporation, Office of the Comptroller of the Currency, "Federal Bank Regulatory Agencies Issue Interim Final Rule for Money Market Liquidity Facility," joint press release, March 19, 2020, at https://www.federalreserve.gov/newsevents/pressreleases/monetary20200319a.htm.

debt or corporate debt exchange-traded funds on secondary markets.[12] Both facilities will purchase debt through an SPV. Both facilities can only purchase debt that is investment grade or issued by investment-grade issuers. The issuer must have material operations in the United States and cannot receive direct federal financial assistance related to COVID-19. For the SMCCF, bonds will be purchased at fair market value and must mature in five years or less. For the PMCCF, interest rates will be "informed by market rates," and borrowers will pay a one percentage point commitment fee. The borrower may call any bond at par in the future, enabling the facility to wind down more quickly if financial conditions normalize. Both programs are currently scheduled to terminate at the end of September 2020.

- **Term Asset-Backed Securities Loan Facility (TALF).** The Fed revived the TALF to make nonrecourse, three-year loans to private investors through a SPV to purchase newly issued, highly rated ABS backed by various nonmortgage loans.[13] Eligible ABS include those backed by certain auto loans, student loans, credit card receivables, equipment loans, floorplan loans, insurance premium finance loans, small business loans guaranteed by the Small Business Administration, or servicing advance receivables. Any company with an account with a primary dealer would be eligible for a TALF loan. Borrowers would pay an interest rate that would be one or two percentage points above a LIBOR swap rate and a fee equal to 0.1% of the loan amount. The Fed bears the risk that the value of the ABS falls below the loan amount plus a haircut. Borrowers may prepay the loan. The program is currently scheduled to terminate at the end of September 2020.

The CPFF, PDCF, and TALF are very similar to the 2008 facilities discussed below. The MMLF is very similar to the 2008 Asset-Backed Commercial Paper Money Market Mutual Fund Liquidity Facility (AMLF) but accepts a wider range of collateral than the AMLF accepted in 2008. The PMCCF and SMCCF are unlike any 2008 facilities.

The potential size of these programs is generally limited only by participants' pre-crisis borrowing patterns; the Fed has virtually unlimited ability to fund them. The risk posed to the Fed (and ultimately, the taxpayer) through these facilities is hard to quantify given the uncertainty surrounding COVID-19, but risk is mitigated because the credit is collateralized and borrowers must qualify based on terms such as credit ratings. In addition, Treasury has pledged $10 billion of assets from the Exchange Stabilization Fund for each of these facilities except the PDCF to protect the Fed from future losses—although these losses would still be borne by the federal government.[14] Each facility was approved by the Treasury Secretary.

Amounts outstanding through 13(3) programs are reported weekly on the Fed's balance sheet.[15] More detailed information is provided in the Fed's Quarterly Report on Federal Reserve Balance

---

[12] Federal Reserve, "Federal Reserve Announces Extensive New Measures To Support The Economy," press release, March 23, 2020, at https://www.federalreserve.gov/newsevents/pressreleases/monetary20200323b.htm.

[13] Federal Reserve, "Federal Reserve Announces Extensive New Measures To Support The Economy," press release, March 23, 2020, at https://www.federalreserve.gov/newsevents/pressreleases/monetary20200323b.htm.

[14] The ESF was not used to back stop 13(3) programs in 2008, but some programs were backed by other Treasury funds.

[15] Federal Reserve, *Factors Affecting Reserve Balances,* Data Release H.4.1, at https://www.federalreserve.gov/releases/h41/.

Sheet Developments.[16] The Dodd-Frank Act requires the Fed to provide the congressional committees of jurisdiction with details of all transactions, including amounts and the identities of borrowers, within 7 days of the program's creation and with updates every 30 days thereafter. In addition, the Dodd-Frank Act requires transaction details to be publicly disclosed one year after the facility is closed.[17] See the section below entitled "Oversight Requirements" for more details.

Use of Section 13(3) in 2008

Section 13(3) was used to authorize multiple actions taken by the Fed when financial conditions worsened at two points in 2008—around the time the investment bank Bear Stearns experienced difficulties in March and following the failure of the investment bank Lehman Brothers in September. Credit extended under Section 13(3) in 2008 can be divided into two broad categories:

1. broadly based facilities to address liquidity problems in specific markets and
2. exclusive, tailored assistance to prevent the disorderly failure of individual firms deemed too big to fail.[18]

Credit outstanding (in the form of cash or securities) under Section 13(3) peaked at $710 billion in November 2008.[19] Currently, all credit extended under Section 13(3) has been repaid with interest and all 13(3) facilities have expired.[20] Contrary to popular belief, the Fed did not suffer any losses on transactions taken under Section 13(3) and earned profits of more than $30 billion (more than half of which is AIG[21] related).[22] Nevertheless, some of these transactions exposed the taxpayer to greater ex ante risks than the discount window because the terms of the programs had fewer safeguards—in some cases involving nonrecourse loans[23] and troubled asset purchases, for example. The next two sections summarize this experience, with more detail provided in the **Appendix**.[24]

---

[16] Available at https://www.federalreserve.gov/monetarypolicy/quarterly-balance-sheet-developments-report.htm.

[17] Transaction data is posted at https://www.federalreserve.gov/newsevents/reform_transaction.htm.

[18] For more information, see CRS Report R42150, *Systemically Important or "Too Big to Fail" Financial Institutions*, by Marc Labonte.

[19] Total does not include asset guarantees for Citigroup and Bank of America, under which funds were never used.

[20] One facility, Maiden Lane I, still held more than $1 billion of assets at the end of 2014. It has no debt and is not authorized to purchase additional assets.

[21] In addition to the $30 billion in net income received by the Fed, Treasury received an additional $17.6 billion as net income on the sale of equity that the Fed originally received (and subsequently transferred to the Treasury) as recompense for the Fed's loan to AIG.

[22] Profits are defined here as payments received in excess of principal outlayed. It does not net out administrative expenses, which are not reported separately for each facility. This report does not consider whether the Fed earned economic profits on these transactions. For example, the income from these transactions may have been partially offset by lost income if the Fed offset those facilities by holding fewer Treasury securities on its balance sheet. One study attempts to estimate this effect for the Fed's broadly based facilities (but not for its special assistance to firms deemed "too big to fail.") For Section 13(3) facilities, it estimates that the facilities earned $8.1 billion in interest and fee income, but the "cost of funds" for those programs was $1.1 billion, so the Fed earned $7 billion net income over the life of the programs. See Michael Fleming and Nicholas Klagge, "Income Effects of Federal Reserve Liquidity Facilities," Federal Reserve Bank of New York, *Current Issues in Economics and Finance*, vol. 17, no. 1, 2011, at http://www.nyfedeconomists.org/research/current_issues/ci17-1.pdf.

[23] Under a non-recourse loan, the creditor has no right to seek payment beyond the collateral posted in the event that the loan is not repaid.

[24] For more information, see Federal Reserve, Office of the Inspector General, *The Federal Reserve's Section 13(3)*

Lessons From the 2008 Experience

As this report discusses, the 2008 experience with 13(3) facilities yields a few insights that may be applicable to its use in 2020.

- Financial turmoil creates liquidity (cash flow) and solvency (negative net worth) problems for financial firms. The Fed is designed to address liquidity problems but not solvency problems. In 2008, Congress created the Troubled Asset Relief Program (TARP) to address solvency problems.[25]

- The Fed can quickly ramp up lending once a facility is established. Most programs were created between September and November 2008. Outstanding credit under 13(3) exceeded $700 billion by November 2008.

- In hindsight, the 2008 liquidity facilities did not prove to be as risky as they appeared. All facilities yielded positive net income for the Fed, and none suffered any defaults. Credit outstanding wound down relatively quickly once financial conditions normalized.

- Statutory restrictions in Section 13(3) were less restrictive than they appeared. For example, these restrictions would seem to limit the Fed to lending, but asset purchases were possible through LLCs or special purpose vehicles (SPVs) created and controlled by the Fed.

- The Fed would frequently include size limits and termination dates when new facilities were announced, but these would typically be revised as circumstances changed.

- When borrowers must apply to access funding, take-up rates can fall short of policymakers' goals. For example, the Term Asset-Backed Securities Loan Facility (TALF) was envisioned as a $1 trillion program by Treasury, but it peaked at $48 billion.

- The financial crisis marked a turning point in the Fed's image with the public and its relationship with Congress, arguably in large part due to its emergency facilities. In response, the Fed took many steps to become more transparent. The Dodd-Frank Act created new restrictions on Section 13(3) lending. In particular, it tried to prevent "bailouts" of failing firms.

- The confidential nature of the facilities were particularly unpopular with some. This led to requirements in the Dodd-Frank Act that the identities of borrowers be publicly disclosed after a lag. Such disclosure risks creating a stigma that may cause borrowers to be reluctant to use facilities for fear that creditors perceive them as troubled. This stigma risks undermining the goal of the facilities—to restore or maintain financial stability. Stigma was largely not a problem in 2008, but unlike then, borrowers now know that their confidentiality will not be maintained.

Broadly Based Facilities

The Fed created six broadly based facilities under Section 13(3) in 2008 to extend credit to all eligible borrowers within a particular class of nonbank financial firms or to a particular segment of financial markets:

- **Term Securities Lending Facility (TSLF) and Primary Dealer Credit Facility (PDCF).** The TSLF and PDCF were created to assist primary dealers. The Fed made short-term loans through the PDCF and TSLF to primary dealers to ensure that other primary dealers did not experience liquidity crises in the wake of the primary dealer Bear Stearns's financial difficulties.

Lending Facilities to Support Overall Market Liquidity, November 2010, at http://oig.federalreserve.gov/reports/ FRS_Lending_Facilities_Report_final-11-23-10_web.pdf. See also U.S. Government Accountability Office (GAO), *Federal Reserve System: Opportunities Exist to Strengthen Policies and Processes for Managing Emergency Assistance*, GAO-11-696, July 21, 2011, at http://www.gao.gov/new.items/d11696.pdf. The Fed was required to report to Congress on assistance provided pursuant to Section 13(3); these reports are posted at http://www.federalreserve.gov/monetarypolicy/bst_reports.htm. See also the Fed's website *Credit and Liquidity Programs and the Balance Sheet*, available at http://www.federalreserve.gov/monetarypolicy/bst_archive.htm.

[25] For more information, see CRS Report R41427, *Troubled Asset Relief Program (TARP): Implementation and Status*, by Baird Webel.

- **Asset-Backed Commercial Paper Money Market Mutual Fund Liquidity Facility (AMLF), Commercial Paper Funding Facility (CPFF), and Money Market Investor Funding Facility (MMIFF).** The AMLF, CPFF, and MMIFF were created to support the commercial paper market (the MMIFF was never used). The Fed set up its commercial paper facilities after a run on money market mutual funds forced the latter to contract their large holdings of commercial paper.

- **Term Asset-Backed Securities Loan Facility (TALF).** The TALF was created to support the ABS market. Through TALF, the Fed made three- and five-year loans to private investors to encourage them to purchase ABS other than residential mortgage-backed securities (MBS).[26] ABS are an alternative way that banks and nonbanks finance loans to consumers and businesses, and they are often referred to as a form of *shadow banking*—activities that substitute for traditional bank lending and deposit-taking.[27] The decline in the value and liquidity of ABS during the crisis resulted in a sharp contraction in their issuance, reducing the credit available to households and businesses.

Table 1 provides a summary of the terms and uses of these facilities. All the facilities except for TALF were used to provide short-term liquidity—conceptually comparable to the role of the discount window. The CPFF was the largest facility, and TALF was the smallest. As can be seen in the table, none of these facilities extended credit after 2010.

---

[26] Other Federal Reserve and federal emergency programs beyond the scope of this report were aimed at supporting mortgage-backed securities (MBS).

[27] For more information, see CRS Report R43345, *Shadow Banking: Background and Policy Issues*, by Edward V. Murphy.

Table 1. Broadly Based Facilities Created in 2008 Under Section 13(3)

	Usage			Terms and Conditions			
Facility	Loans Outstanding at Peak	Total Income	Number of Participants	Lending Rate/Fee	Recourse/ Haircut	Term	Date Announced-Expired
Term Securities Lending Facility (TSLF)	$235.5 billion on Oct. 1, 2008	$0.8 billion	18	Set at auction, with minimum fee of 10 to 25 basis points	Yes/Yes	28 days	Mar. 11, 2008-Feb. 1, 2010
Primary Dealer Credit Facility (PDCF)	$146.6 billion on Oct. 1, 2008	$0.6 billion	18	Rate set equal to Fed's discount rate; fees of up to 40 basis points for frequent users	Yes/Yes	overnight	Mar. 16, 2008-Feb. 1, 2010
Asset-Backed Commercial Paper Money Market Mutual Fund Liquidity Facility (AMLF)	$152.1 billion on Oct. 1, 2008	$0.5 billion	11 from 7 bank holding companies	Fed's discount rate	No/No	120 or 270 days	Sept. 19, 2008-Feb. 1, 2010
Commercial Paper Funding Facility (CPFF)	$348.2 billion on Jan. 21, 2009	$6.1 billion	120	Markups of 100 to 300 basis points over overnight index swap rate; fees of 10 to 100 basis points	No/No	90 days	Oct. 7, 2008-Feb. 1, 2010
Term Asset-Backed Securities Loan Facility (TALF)	$48.2 billion on Mar. 17, 2010	$1.6 billion to Fed; $0.7 billion to Treasury	177	Various markups over LIBOR or federal funds rate; 10 to 20 basis point administrative fee	No/Yes	5 years for CMBS, 3 years for other	Nov. 25, 2008- Mar. 31, 2010 (June 30, 2010, for new CMBS)

Sources: Federal Reserve, Office of the Inspector General, *The Federal Reserve's Section 13(3) Lending Facilities to Support Overall Market Liquidity*, November 2010; Federal Reserve, *Quarterly Report on Federal Reserve Balance Sheet Developments*, various dates. U.S. Government Accountability Office, *Federal Reserve System: Opportunities Exist to Strengthen Policies and Processes for Managing Emergency Assistance*, GAO-11-696, July 21, 2011.

Notes: Expiration date for facilities marks date after which no new activities were authorized. For some facilities, existing loans remained outstanding after the expiration date. Some facilities did not begin operations on the date announced. Recourse only includes to participant's assets; the Fed had recourse for AMLF and TALF only in the case of material misrepresentation.

Figure 1 plots loans outstanding for these five facilities from March 2008, when the first facility was created, to October 2014, when the last loan was repaid. Usage of the facilities spiked beginning in mid-September 2008, peaked in December 2008, and then tapered off relatively quickly in 2009 as financial conditions stabilized. From 2010 to 2014, there were only residual amounts of credit outstanding through TALF. According to GAO, use of the facilities was relatively concentrated among a small number of borrowers—which may reflect concentration in those markets.[28]

Figure 1. Loans Outstanding Under Broadly Based Facilities

(March 2008-October 2014)

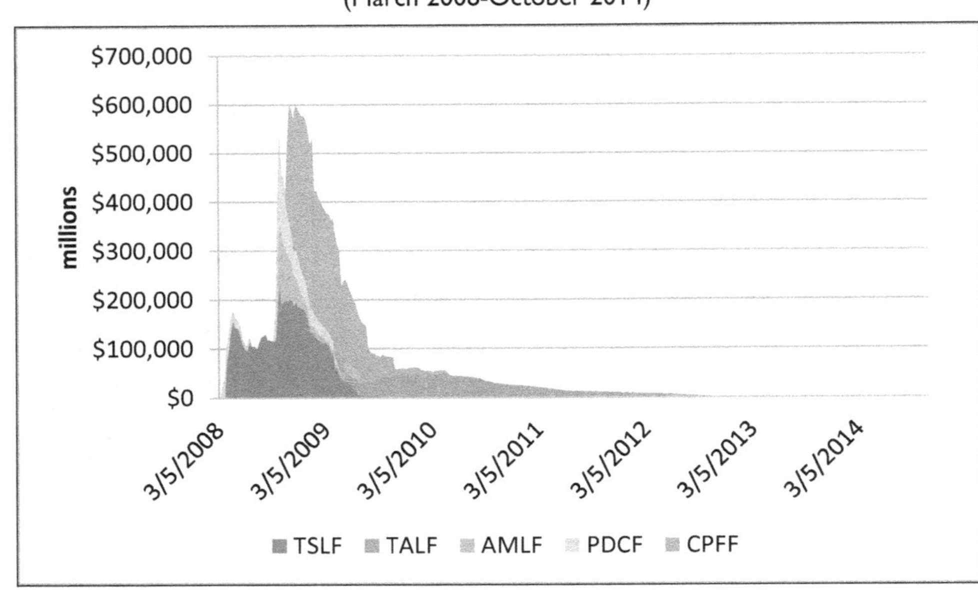

Source: Federal Reserve, H.4.1 release, various dates.

Notes: For TSLF, lending took the form of Treasury securities. For CPFF, commercial paper was purchased. For other facilities, lending took the form of cash. See **Appendix** for details.

Special Assistance to Firms Deemed "Too Big to Fail"

Section 13(3) was also invoked to provide exclusive, tailored assistance to prevent the disorderly failure of four large financial firms on an ad hoc basis:

- In March 2008, the Fed assisted JP Morgan Chase's takeover of Bear Stearns to prevent the latter's failure. Assistance was provided through first, a short-term bridge loan and then, the purchase of Bear Stearns troubled assets, financed through a $29 billion Fed loan;

- In September 2008, the Fed prevented AIG's failure by initially providing it a line of credit of $85 billion. The assistance was restructured several times, with the loan eventually replaced by a Fed pledge to purchase up to $52.5 billion in troubled assets in November (and the rest of the assistance shifted to Treasury);

---

[28] U.S. Government Accountability Office, *Federal Reserve System: Opportunities Exist to Strengthen Policies and Processes for Managing Emergency Assistance*, GAO-11-696, July 21, 2011, Tables 12, 20, 25, 27, 31, at http://www.gao.gov/new.items/d11696.pdf.

- In November 2008, the Fed, Treasury, and the Federal Deposit Insurance Cooperation (FDIC) announced a joint agreement to guarantee a more than $300 billion portfolio of Citigroup's troubled assets;
- In January 2009, the Fed, Treasury, and FDIC announced a joint agreement to guarantee a $118 billion portfolio of Bank of America's troubled assets to assist its takeover of Merrill Lynch. (The agreement was never finalized.)

These actions were motivated by concerns that the failure of any of these firms would increase financial instability—in other words, the Fed viewed the firms as too big to fail or too interconnected to fail.[29] In all four cases, the Fed did not limit its action to those of a traditional lender of last resort because problems at the firms were not limited to a need for short-term liquidity. In the Fed's view, the firms were not insolvent, but were vulnerable to losing access to funding markets which could cause their failure.[30] An evaluation of whether these four institutions were solvent at the time was hampered by the "fog of war"—the Fed was forced to judge their solvency hastily in the context of a crisis, in which the value of all assets was rapidly declining and it was uncertain whether the decline was temporary or permanent. While some have described this assistance as a bail out of failing firms, in all four cases, there was not clear evidence that the firms were insolvent in the classic sense.[31] In the case of Bear Stearns, JP Morgan Chase was willing to pay more to acquire it than the value of the Fed's assistance, but later reported losses related to the transaction.[32] The other three firms all eventually returned to profitability once the crisis had ended, which means they may or may not have been solvent at the time of the intervention.

As notable as whom the Fed assisted is whom it chose not to assist—Lehman Brothers. Although Lehman Brothers was an investment firm similar to Bear Stearns, the Fed chose not to help facilitate its takeover by Barclays. Instead, Lehman Brothers filed for bankruptcy. Then-Chairman Bernanke later testified that the Fed declined to assist Lehman Brothers because it held inadequate collateral[33]—although some of the Fed's other interventions under Section 13(3) featured concerns about inadequate collateral. While one cannot say what would have happened in the counterexample where the Fed had assisted Lehman Brothers, Lehman Brothers' failure marked the worsening of the financial crisis.

Troubled assets were purchased from Bear Stearns and AIG through three limited liability corporations (LLCs) created and controlled by the Fed named Maiden Lane. **Figure 2** shows loans outstanding to the Maiden Lanes and directly to AIG. The direct loan to AIG was paid off in 2011. The asset holdings and loans of the Maiden Lanes tapered off slowly until 2011, when the pace accelerated. The final Maiden Lane loan was fully repaid in 2012; final profits to the Fed will not be known until residual asset holdings are extinguished. Although Citigroup and Bank of

---

[29] For more information, see CRS Report R42150, *Systemically Important or "Too Big to Fail" Financial Institutions*, by Marc Labonte.

[30] As described in the reports pursuant to Section 129, available at http://www.federalreserve.gov/monetarypolicy/ bst_reports.htm. In the case of Bank of America, losses were greatest at Merrill Lynch, which Bank of America was in the process of acquiring. The Fed (and Treasury) may have been most concerned that if Bank of America was not offered special assistance, the merger would fall through and Merrill Lynch would experience a disorderly failure.

[31] The solvency of Bear Stearns and AIG is analyzed in William Cline and Joseph Gagnon, *Lehman Died, Bagehot Lives: Why Did the Fed and Treasury Let a Major Wall Street Bank Fail?*, Peterson Institute for International Economics, Policy Brief no. PB 13-21, at http://www.piie.com/publications/pb/pb13-21.pdf.

[32] "JPMorgan Took a Bath on Bear Stearns Sale: Dimon," *Reuters*, October 10, 2012, at http://www.cnbc.com/id/ 49361397/.

[33] Chairman Ben S. Bernanke, Remarks before the Committee on Banking, Housing, and Urban Affairs, U.S. Senate September 23, 2008, available at http://www.federalreserve.gov/newsevents/testimony/bernanke20080923a1.htm.

America were banks, this assistance was nevertheless authorized under Section 13(3) because it took the form of asset guarantees. The guarantees to Citigroup and Bank of America are not shown in **Figure 2** because Fed funds were never extended under those guarantees.

Figure 2. Loans Outstanding for Special Assistance

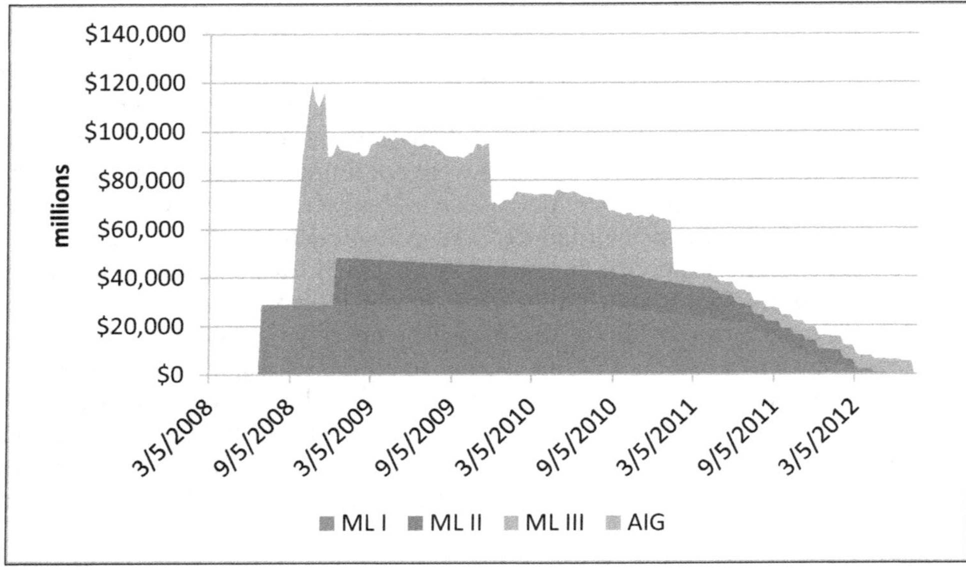

Source: Federal Reserve, H.4.1 release, various dates.

Notes: ML I = Maiden Lane I, facility to assist the takeover of Bear Stearns; ML II = Maiden Lane II, facility to assist AIG; ML III = Maiden Lane III, facility to assist AIG; AIG = direct loan from Fed to AIG. Funds were never extended under asset guarantee to Citigroup and Bank of America.

Limits on Emergency Lending

Under normal authority, the Fed faces statutory limitations on whom it may lend to, what it may accept as collateral, and for how long it may lend.[34] If the Fed wishes to extend credit that does not meet these criteria, it can initiate assistance under Section 13(3).

Restrictions on Emergency Lending in Place in 2008

Section 13(3) was not in the original Federal Reserve Act of 1913; it was added in 1932 (47 Stat 715). Until the Dodd-Frank Act, the authority was very broad, with few limitations. It required that[35]

---

[34] For more information on the discount window, see https://www.frbdiscountwindow.org/en/Pages/General-Information/The-Discount-Window.aspx.

[35] The interpretation of the statute that follows each bullet is based on Alexander Mehra, "Legal Authority in Unusual and Exigent Circumstances: The Federal Reserve and the Financial Crisis," *University Of Pennsylvania Journal of Business Law*, vol. 13, no. 1, pp. 221-227.

- at least five of the seven Fed governors find that there are "unusual and exigent circumstances"[36]—while this phrase has no specific legal definition, it implies that financial conditions are not normal;[37]

- the Fed may "discount (for) any individual, partnership, or corporation"—that is, assistance should take the form of a loan, and the loan may be made to private individuals or businesses;

- the borrower must present "notes, drafts, and bills of exchange endorsed or otherwise secured to the satisfaction of the Federal Reserve Bank"—that is, the loan must be backed by collateral approved by the Fed;[38]

- the Fed shall charge an interest rate consistent with the same limitations applied to the discount window;[39] and

- "the Federal Reserve Bank shall obtain evidence that such individual, partnership, or corporation is unable to secure adequate credit accommodations from other banking institutions"—that is, there must be evidence that the borrower does not have private alternatives.

These restrictions did not prevent the Fed from taking several unorthodox actions in 2008. Notably, in some cases, "In form, these transactions were structured as loans. But in substance, they permitted the Fed to move assets off the balance sheets of these institutions and onto its own."[40] In the cases of AIG and Bear Stearns, the Fed purchased their assets through limited liability corporations that it created and controlled (called Maiden Lane I, II, and III). This structure allowed the Fed to comply with Section 13(3) because the asset purchases were financed through loans from the Fed to the Maiden Lanes. The loans were backed by those assets and were eventually repaid when the assets were sold off or matured.[41] In the cases of Citigroup and Bank of America, the firms were offered a guarantee in the event that they suffered losses on a portfolio of assets, structured as a loan "provided ... on a nonrecourse basis, except with respect to interest

---

[36] Unusual and exigent circumstances is not defined, but is considered a high threshold. See Alexander Mehra, "Legal Authority in Unusual and Exigent Circumstances: The Federal Reserve and the Financial Crisis," *University Of Pennsylvania Journal of Business Law*, vol. 13, no. 1, pp. 221-227, citing Thomas C. Baxter, Jr., general counsel, Fed. Reserve Bank of N.Y., "The Legal Position of the Central Bank, The Case of the Federal Reserve Bank of New York," January 19, 2009, available at https://www.google.com/search?q= thomas+c.+Baxter%2C+Jr.%2C+The+Legal+Position+of+the+Central+bank&ie=utf-8&oe=utf-8.

[37] If five governors are not available, the decision can be made unanimously by the governors available (12 U.S.C. 248r). On at least one occasion in 2008, because of vacancies on the Federal Reserve Board action under Section 13(3) was approved with only four governors voting. See Federal Reserve, *Report Pursuant to Section 129: Bridge Loan to The Bear Stearns Companies*, at http://www.federalreserve.gov/monetarypolicy/files/129bearstearnsbridgeloan.pdf; Federal Open Market Committee, *Conference Call of the Federal Open Market Committee on March 10, 2008*, at http://www.federalreserve.gov/monetarypolicy/files/FOMC20080310confcall.pdf.

[38] According to a working paper by legal counsel at the Fed, this requirement placed "virtually no restrictions on the form a written credit instrument must take in order to be eligible for discount." David H. Small and James A. Clouse, "The Scope of Monetary Policy Actions Authorized under the Federal Reserve Act," Federal Reserve, working paper, July 19, 2004, p. 15.

[39] The discount window standards referenced here state that rates shall be "fixed with a view of accommodating commerce and business" (12 U.S.C. 357).

[40] Alexander Mehra, "Legal Authority in Unusual and Exigent Circumstances: The Federal Reserve and the Financial Crisis," *University Of Pennsylvania Journal of Business Law*, vol. 13, no. 1, p. 235. This article also presents arguments that the Fed nevertheless exceeded its legal authority for some transactions under Section 13(3).

[41] The Commercial Paper Funding Facility (CPFF) was also structured as a limited liability corporation (LLC) that purchased commercial paper and was financed by loans from the Fed. The Fed also created LLCs associated with the Term Asset-Backed Securities Loan Facility (TALF).

payments and fees."[42] The Fed also made a loan directly to AIG backed by the company's general assets, meaning there were no specific securities pledged in the event of nonpayment.[43] Furthermore, the Fed has interpreted "unusual and exigent circumstances" to mean that assistance should be temporary, but routinely extended each facility's expiration date until demand for credit had waned.

One statutory revision to Section 13(3) affected the Fed's actions in 2008. In 1991, the Federal Deposit Insurance Corporation Improvement Act (P.L. 102-242; 12 U.S.C. 1811) contained a provision that removed the requirement that collateral be "of the kind and maturities made eligible for discount for member banks" at the discount window. According to the sponsor, Senator Christopher Dodd, the rationale for the provision was to enable the Fed "to make fully secured loans to securities firms in instances similar to the 1987 stock market crash."[44] Securities firms, it was argued, would not necessarily hold the same sort of assets that banks used as collateral at the discount window. By removing this language, the Fed had discretion to lend against a broader array of assets.

Changes in the Dodd-Frank Act

Concerns in Congress about some of the Fed's actions under Section 13(3) during the financial crisis led to the section's amendment in Section 1101 of the Dodd-Frank Act. Generally, the intention of the provision in the Dodd-Frank Act was to prevent the Fed from bailing out failing firms while preserving enough of its discretion that it could still create broadly based facilities to address unpredictable market-access problems during a crisis.[45] Specifically, the Dodd-Frank Act

- replaced "individual, partnership, or corporation" with "participant in any program or facility with broad-based eligibility";

- required that assistance be "for the purpose of providing liquidity to the financial system, and not to aid a failing financial company." It ruled out lending to an insolvent firm, defined as in any bankruptcy, resolution, or insolvency proceeding;

- required that loans be secured "sufficient(ly) to protect taxpayers from losses," and that collateral be assigned a "lendable value" that is "consistent with sound risk management practices";

- forbade "a program or facility that is structured to remove assets from the balance sheet of a single and specific company";

- required any program "to be terminated in a timely and orderly fashion"; and

- required the "prior approval of the Secretary of the Treasury."[46]

---

[42] Federal Reserve, *Report Pursuant to Section 129: Authorization to Provide Residual Financing to Bank of America Corporation*, January 15, 2009, at http://www.federalreserve.gov/monetarypolicy/files/129bofa.pdf.

[43] Federal Reserve, *Report Pursuant to Section 129: Secured Credit Facility Authorized for American International Group*, September 16, 2008, at http://www.federalreserve.gov/monetarypolicy/files/129aigseccreditfacility.pdf.

[44] Senator Christopher Dodd, *Congressional Record*, November 27, 1991, p. 36131. See also Walker Todd, "FDICIA's Emergency Liquidity Provisions," Federal Reserve Bank of Cleveland, *Economic Review*, Third Quarter, 1993.

[45] See, for example, the *Joint Explanatory Statement of the Committee of the Conference to* P.L. 111-203, H.Rept. 111-517, 111th Congress, June 29, 2010.

[46] The Dodd-Frank Act left three requirements in the original statute largely unchanged: (1) a finding of unusual and exigent circumstances; (2) that interest rates be set consistent with statute governing the discount window; and (3) a finding that the borrower be unable to access private credit.

Proponents of the Dodd-Frank Act believed that the Fed's authority to provide assistance to too big to fail firms was no longer necessary because of other changes in the act. The Fed justified its special assistance to too big to fail firms during the crisis on the grounds that these firms could not be wound down without causing financial instability under existing law because of perceived shortcomings of the bankruptcy process. Fed officials called for the creation of a resolution regime for non-banks modeled on the FDIC's bank resolution regime so that such assistance would not be necessary in the future.[47] Title II of the Dodd-Frank Act created such a regime, called the "Orderly Liquidation Authority."[48] While critics oppose Title II for reasons beyond the scope of this report, proponents of the Dodd-Frank Act argue that eliminating the Fed's ability to prevent firms from failing under Section 13(3) will not result in financial instability now that firms can undergo an orderly resolution under Title II. According to Ben Bernanke, chairman of the Fed during the financial crisis, "With the creation of the [orderly] liquidation authority, the ability of the Fed to make loans to individual troubled firms like Bear [Stearns] and AIG was no longer needed and, appropriately, was eliminated."[49]

The Fed's Rule Implementing the Dodd-Frank Act's Changes

As Section 13(3) can be used only in "unusual and exigent circumstances" and had not been used for decades, the Fed had not promulgated a rule governing its use as of 2008, even though it had the discretion to do so. The Dodd-Frank Act also required the Fed to promulgate a rule implementing Section 1101 "as soon as is practicable," and the Fed issued a proposed rule doing so in 2013.[50] Some public comments criticized the rule for not adding meaningful quantitative or qualitative definitions to the terms "unusual and exigent circumstances," collateral, penalty rate, insolvency, broadly based, or the duration of assistance.[51] Generally, critics believe that the vagueness of the rule is undesirable for the same reason that proponents view it as desirable— because it maximize the Fed's future discretion.[52]

On December 18, 2015, the Fed promulgated a final rule implementing Section 1101.[53] Compared with the proposed rule, the final rule provided more specificity as to how the Fed would comply with the Dodd-Frank Act's requirements, and thus gives the Fed less discretion. For example, the final rule requires lending to be at a "penalty rate," which it defines as a premium to the market rate prevailing in normal circumstances. In some cases, the final rule goes beyond the statutory requirements. For example, statute only prohibits lending to firms that are in a bankruptcy or insolvency proceeding, whereas the final rule also prohibits lending to any facility unless it is open to at least five eligible borrowers, any recipient who has not been current on its debt over the past 90 days, a healthy firm for the purposes of preventing a third party from failing (as was

---

[47] See, for example, Chairman Ben S. Bernanke, "Federal Reserve Programs To Strengthen Credit Markets And The Economy," Testimony Before the Committee on Financial Services, U.S. House of Representatives, February 10, 2009, at http://www.federalreserve.gov/newsevents/testimony/bernanke20090210a.htm.

[48] For more information, see the FDIC website https://www.fdic.gov/resauthority/.

[49] Ben Bernanke, "Warren-Vitter and the Lender of Last Resort," Brookings Institution, blog, May 15, 2015, at http://www.brookings.edu/blogs/ben-bernanke/posts/2015/05/15-warren-vitter-proposal.

[50] Federal Reserve, "Federal Reserve Board Seeks Comment on Proposed Amendments to Regulation A Regarding Emergency Lending Authority," press release, December 23, 2013, at http://www.federalreserve.gov/newsevents/press/bcreg/20131223a.htm. For more information, see CRS Legal Sidebar WSLG1247, *Fed's Emergency Lending Rule Not Finalized A Year After Public Comment Period*, by M. Maureen Murphy (no longer distributable).

[51] Comment letters are posted on the Fed's website at http://www.federalreserve.gov/apps/foia/ViewComments.aspx?doc_id=R-1476&doc_ver=1.

[52] This debate is discussed below in the section entitled "How Much Discretion Should the Fed Be Granted?"

[53] Federal Reserve, "Extensions of Credit by Federal Reserve Banks," 80 *Federal Register* 78959, December 18, 2015, available at https://www.gpo.gov/fdsys/pkg/FR-2015-12-18/pdf/2015-30584.pdf.

---

the case with JP Morgan Chase and Bear Stearns), and a firm so that it can avoid bankruptcy or resolution. **Table 2** explains how the final rule implements the major provisions of Section 13(3).

Table 2. Major Provisions of the Fed's Final Rule Implementing Dodd-Frank Act Changes to Section 13(3)

Section 13(3) Provision	Final Rule Implementation
Limits assistance to any "participant in any program or facility with broad-based eligibility."	Minimum of five eligible participants for a program to meet the "broad-based eligibility" requirement.
Specifies that assistance be "for the purpose of providing liquidity to the financial system, and not to aid a failing financial company." Requires that regulations preclude insolvent borrowers, i.e., borrowers "in bankruptcy, resolution ... or any other Federal or State insolvency proceeding."	Specifies that liquidity may be provided only to an identifiable market or sector of the financial system. Provides that a program may not be used for a firm to avoid bankruptcy or resolution. Specifies that a program designed to aid one or more failing companies or to assist one or more companies to avoid bankruptcy, resolution, or insolvency will not be considered to have the required "broad-based eligibility." Requires borrowers be current on their debt for 90 days before borrowing. Permits the Fed to determine whether the applicant is insolvent. Excludes a firm from borrowing from Fed if the purpose is to help a third-party firm that is insolvent. Includes immediate repayment and enforcement actions for firms that "make[s] a willful misrepresentation regarding its solvency." Specifies that the Fed is under no obligation to extend credit to a borrower.
Requires that loans be secured "sufficient[ly] to protect taxpayers from losses," and collateral be assigned a "lendable value" that is "consistent with sound risk management practices."	Requires that the Fed assign a lendable value to collateral at the time credit is extended.
Forbids "a program or facility that is structured to remove assets from the balance sheet of a single and specific company."	Prohibits removing assets from one or more firms that meet the rule's definition of failing.
Requires "prior approval of the Secretary of the Treasury."	Specifies that no program may be established without the approval of the Secretary of the Treasury.
Specifies that the authority may be invoked only in "unusual and exigent circumstances" and that any program be "terminated in a timely and orderly fashion."	Requires that the Fed provide "a description of the unusual and exigent circumstances that exist" no later than 7 days after establishing a program. Requires that initial credit terminate within one year, with extension possible only upon a vote of five governors and approval by the Secretary of the Treasury. Requires a review of programs every six months to assure timely termination.
Specifies that rates be consistent with the statutory requirements governing the discount rate.[a]	Requires the rate charged must be a "penalty rate," defined as a rate that is a premium to the market rate in normal circumstances. It must also be a rate that "affords liquidity in unusual and exigent circumstances; and ... encourages repayment of the credit and discourages use of the program" when "economic conditions normalize." Permits the charging of "any fees, penalties,...or other consideration...to protect and appropriately compensate the taxpayer.... "

Section 13(3) Provision	Final Rule Implementation
Specifies that the borrower must be "unable to secure adequate credit accommodations from other banking institutions."[a]	Requires evidence of inability of participants in a program to obtain credit. The evidence may be based on economic conditions in a particular market or markets; on the borrower's certification of its inability "to secure adequate credit accommodations from other banking institutions," or on "other evidence from participants or other sources."

Source: CRS based on Federal Reserve, "Extensions of Credit by Federal Reserve Banks," 80 *Federal Register* 78959, December 18, 2015, available at https://www.gpo.gov/fdsys/pkg/FR-2015-12-18/pdf/2015-30584.pdf.

a. Requirement is largely unchanged by the Dodd-Frank Act.

Oversight Requirements

Following the use of Section 13(3) in 2008, three laws have been enacted affecting congressional oversight of emergency lending.

First, in 2008, Section 129 of the Emergency Economic Stabilization Act (P.L. 110-343) required the Fed to report to the congressional committees of jurisdiction on the terms of and justification for assistance within seven days of providing assistance under Section 13(3), with updates every 60 days.[54]

Second, in 2009, an amendment to the Helping Families Save Their Homes Act (Section 801 of P.L. 111-22) included a provision that allows Government Accountability Office (GAO) audits of "any action taken by the Board under ... Section 13(3) of the Federal Reserve Act with respect to a single and specific partnership or corporation." This provision allowed GAO audits of the Maiden Lane facilities and the asset guarantees of Citigroup and Bank of America, but it maintained audit restrictions on non-emergency activities and the broadly based emergency lending facilities.

Third, Section 1101 of the Dodd-Frank Act required that details on the assistance provided under Section 13(3) be reported to the committees of jurisdiction within seven days, with regular updates. Section 1103 required lending records (including details on the identity of the borrower and the terms of the loan) from the crisis to be publicly released on December 1, 2010,[55] and lending records from future programs created under Section 13(3) to be publicly released a year after the facility was terminated or two years after lending ceased, whichever came first. Section 1102 allowed GAO to audit any action under Section 13(3) for operational integrity, accounting, financial reporting, internal controls, effectiveness of collateral policies, favoritism, and use of third-party contractors—but did not allow GAO to conduct an economic evaluation—and Section 1109 required GAO to conduct an audit of all Fed emergency facilities created between December 2007 and enactment.[56] GAO may not disclose confidential information until the lending records are released.

For more details, see CRS Report R42079, *Federal Reserve: Oversight and Disclosure Issues*, by Marc Labonte.

---

[54] These reports are available at http://www.federalreserve.gov/monetarypolicy/bst_reports.htm.

[55] The records can be accessed at http://www.federalreserve.gov/newsevents/reform_transaction.htm.

[56] The audit is available at U.S. Government Accountability Office, *Federal Reserve System: Opportunities Exist to Strengthen Policies and Processes for Managing Emergency Assistance*, GAO-11-696, July 21, 2011, at http://www.gao.gov/new.items/d11696.pdf.

Policy Issues

Why Was the Fed Established as a "Lender of Last Resort"?

Economists distinguish between liquidity problems and solvency problems facing financial firms. Firms become insolvent when their assets are worth less than their liabilities (e.g., because their assets have fallen in value). Liquidity (i.e., cash flow) problems arise because of the maturity mismatch between a financial firm's long-term assets and short-term liabilities. In any instance where such a mismatch exists, no matter how much liquidity the firm holds, a firm is vulnerable to a loss of liquidity if it cannot roll over its short-term liabilities—even if the firm is solvent. In a crisis, creditors are unable to distinguish between solvent and insolvent firms, so both lose access to liquidity. The classic example of a liquidity crisis is a bank run, in which depositors withdraw their deposits (liabilities) and banks cannot liquidate loans (assets) to meet withdrawals. Holding more cash and fewer loans would make a run less likely but could not completely prevent it, and the unintended consequence would be that loans would be more expensive to customers. The Fed was created as a lender of last resort with this scenario in mind—when its depositors withdrew funds, a bank would be able to pledge its assets at the Fed's discount window in exchange for short-term loans. Because the Fed controls the money supply, it is in a unique position to potentially provide unlimited liquidity. This position enhances its ability to credibly pledge to end financial crises. Given that the Fed can only address liquidity problems, it is not equipped to address solvency problems or crises resulting from solvency problems, however.

One alternative to the Fed acting as a lender of last resort in a crisis is to allow the panic to run its course. This was the approach followed in the nineteenth and early twentieth centuries, until repeated panics resulted in the creation of the Fed. Eventually the panic would subside, but crises can lead to significant contractions in real economic activity and declines in prices. Crises cause economic contractions because financial firms extend less credit to consumers and businesses to hoard liquidity.

Who Should Have Access to the Lender of Last Resort?

Lending to Nonbank Financial Firms?

Do nonbank financial firms also face liquidity problems, and does this justify the Fed's emergency authority? Although only banks accept deposits, many types of financial firms face a maturity mismatch between long-term assets and short-term liabilities. As a result, many types of financial firms are vulnerable to liquidity crises. In 2008, the availability of repurchase agreements (repos) and commercial paper—two prominent types of short-term lending for nonbanks—sharply and suddenly contracted, causing liquidity problems for banks and nonfinancial firms. Thus, some nonbank financial firms could also benefit from access to Fed lending in a liquidity crisis.

Although some nonbank firms could benefit from access to a lender of last resort, policymakers might decide to grant them access only if there is some wider societal benefit to doing so. Such benefits could be because a failure to do so would result in financial instability, through spillover effects (e.g., counterparty exposure), contagion, or the disruption of critical functions within the financial system. Banks provide critical functions through their unique role in the payment system, for example. Nonbanks do not play a similar role in the payment system, although they are important participants in similar markets, such as the repo market, that might also be viewed as critical.[57]

Before 2008, there was some debate about whether nonbank financial firms were systemically important enough that there would be widespread repercussions if they faced a crisis. Likewise, there was some debate about whether a nonbank crisis would significantly affect the availability of credit to consumers and businesses. Over time, the nonbank financial sector has grown in absolute terms and relative to banks. The 2008 experience suggests that a nonbank crisis can be damaging to the availability of credit and the broader financial sector. Thus, the rationale of having a lender of last resort to provide liquidity also extends to parts of the nonbank financial system, although the policy tradeoffs may be different. This raises the question of whether there should be disparate treatment of banks and nonbanks—banks receive continual access to the discount window, whereas any given nonbank receives no access to the Fed in normal conditions and uncertain access to the Fed in unusual and exigent circumstances. Should nonbanks be allowed to be members of the Federal Reserve system to ensure access to the discount window?[58] If so, should they be subject to prudential supervision by the Fed?[59]

Not all uses of Section 13(3) during the crisis were for the purpose of providing short-term liquidity, however. TALF loans had terms of three to five years and were intended to revive long-term consumer and business credit (by increasing the demand for ABS, which might be described as increasing their liquidity). The AIG loan initially had a maturity of two years. The Maiden Lane facilities set up for Bear Stearns and AIG and the asset guarantees for Citigroup and Bank of America were all intended to help those firms with troubled assets. The Dodd-Frank Act now requires that assistance provided under Section 13(3) be "for the purpose of providing liquidity to the financial system, and not to aid a failing financial company."

Lending to Nonfinancial Firms?

Another issue is whether Section 13(3) should ever be used to provide credit to nonfinancial firms. In 2008, the Fed chose to use Section 13(3) to provide credit mainly to financial firms, although nonfinancial firms were eligible to sell their commercial paper to the CPFF. The Dodd-Frank Act limits actions under Section 13(3) to providing liquidity to the financial system, but does not limit participants to financial firms. In the 1930s, emergency loans were made to nonfinancial firms. Although nonfinancial firms might also have liquidity needs,[60] they do not

---

[57] For more information on critical functions, see Financial Stability Oversight Council, "Authority to Require Supervision and Regulation of Certain Nonbank Financial Companies," 77 *Federal Register* 21657, April 11, 2012, at http://www.treasury.gov/initiatives/fsoc/rulemaking/Documents/ Authority%20to%20Require%20Supervision%20and%20Regulation%20of%20Certain%20Nonbank%20Financial%20 Companies.pdf.

[58] Another question raised by the crisis is whether foreign firms should have access to the Fed's broadly based emergency facilities. For each facility, foreign firms were not eligible to participate, but U.S. affiliates of foreign firms or foreign affiliates of U.S. firms were, depending on the facility. Firms with foreign parent companies were large users of some facilities. For example, 59% of credit extended under the CPFF went to U.S. subsidiaries of foreign firms. Source: U.S. Government Accountability Office, *Federal Reserve System: Opportunities Exist to Strengthen Policies and Processes for Managing Emergency Assistance*, GAO-11-696, July 21, 2011, at http://www.gao.gov/new.items/ d11696.pdf, Figure 10.

[59] Firms enter a code of conduct agreement upon registering with the Fed as primary dealers, but the Fed does not regulate them for safety and soundness in their capacity as primary dealers. In the words of the New York Fed, "the nature of its relationship with primary dealers is a counterparty relationship, not a regulatory one." Federal Reserve Bank of New York, *Administration of Relationships with Primary Dealers*, January 2010, at https://www.newyorkfed.org/markets/pridealers_policies.html.

[60] The Fed bought some commercial paper issued by nonfinancial firms through the CPFF. Because commercial paper has short maturities, this action can be characterized as providing liquidity rather than long-term credit.

generally face the maturity mismatch that makes liquidity risk inherent to financial firms. Liquidity problems at nonfinancial firms may also pose less systemic risk than at financial firms because they are less interconnected with the financial system and do not perform critical functions in the financial system.

The advantage of providing long-term credit to nonfinancial firms is that it directly stimulates physical capital investment spending on plant and equipment, which in turn directly stimulates gross domestic product (GDP). A disadvantage is that it is more likely to put the Fed in the position of "picking winners", and the Fed has no expertise in evaluating the creditworthiness of loan proposals. Another disadvantage is the potential that the Fed's lending will "crowd out" private capital. In a liquidity crisis, when the availability of private lending, by definition, is constrained, the likelihood that Fed lending comes at the expense of private lending is lower. By contrast, long-term credit, which will outlast a liquidity crisis, has a greater potential for crowding out.

Lending to Government or Government Chartered Entities?

Another category of firms that Congress might consider whether it wants to make ineligible for assistance under Section 13(3) is entities associated with the government, such as government agencies, government-sponsored enterprises (GSEs), or bridge banks created in an FDIC resolution.[61] Some Members of Congress have also expressed concern that Section 13(3) could be used to assist state or municipal governments. The Fed has never used Section 13(3) for these purposes, although it has purchased agency and GSE debt under its normal authority. Current statute does not explicitly rule it out, although such an action might have trouble meeting the statute's various requirements, such as that the facility be broadly based for the purpose of providing liquidity to the financial system.

Lending to Itself?

During the crisis, the Fed structured many of its transactions under Section 13(3) as loans to an LLC or SPV that it created and controlled. It did so to comply with the Section 13(3) requirement that assistance take the form of a loan. For example, in 2008, the Fed created the Commercial Paper Funding Facility (CPFF) to purchase commercial paper, a debt security that is economically equivalent to a short-term loan from the borrower's perspective. In this case, the Fed was able to purchase commercial paper by setting up an SPV that it controlled and lending the SPV funds to finance the purchases. Some of the commercial paper the CPFF purchased was not collateralized, however, so it was not economically equivalent to a collateralized loan.

These actions raise two policy issues. First, should Section 13(3) be restricted so that the Fed cannot lend to SPVs or LLCs it creates and controls? Second, should Section 13(3) be modified so that the Fed can provide short-term liquidity by purchasing debt securities?[62]

From an economic perspective, whether a company accesses short-term liquidity by taking out a loan or issuing a debt security does not change its purpose. On practical grounds, since financial firms increasingly rely on debt securities for liquidity needs, allowing the Fed to purchase them would make it a more effective lender of last resort. But allowing the Fed to purchase securities

---

[61] Direct lending to the federal government is prohibited by Section 14 of the Federal Reserve Act.

[62] The Fed is allowed to purchase a narrow range of securities under Section 14 of the Federal Reserve Act. Few securities issued by private firms are permitted besides bank acceptances and bills of exchange, subject to limitations. The Fed has purchased neither in modern times. For more information, see David H. Small and James A. Clouse, "The Scope of Monetary Policy Actions Authorized under the Federal Reserve Act," Federal Reserve, working paper, July 19, 2004, Section 3.4.

(directly or through SPVs or LLCs it controls) to provide short-term liquidity faces the "slippery slope" problem. The Fed also used LLCs in the Maiden Lanes case, where the goal was not to provide short-term liquidity but to remove troubled assets from a firm's balance sheet. The Dodd-Frank Act maintained the Fed's ability to create SPVs or LLCs, but prohibits "a program or facility that is structured to remove assets from the balance sheet of a single and specific company." It might be difficult to draw a bright line between debt securities purchased for liquidity purposes and other types of securities.

What Are the Potential Costs of Emergency Assistance?

Potential costs inherent in Section 13(3) lending can be divided into risks to taxpayers and broader economic consequences. These costs can be weighed against the benefits of Section 13(3) lending, which could be significant if the lending restores or maintains financial stability. While lending poses risks to the taxpayer, if the Fed did not act, the economic losses from allowing a financial crisis to run its course would also pose risks to taxpayers in terms of a larger federal budget deficit and privately through higher unemployment, lost wealth, and so forth.

The risk to the taxpayer of lending is primarily default risk. The Fed can—but is not required to— attach various conditions to its lending to minimize default, including requiring short maturities, collateral in excess of the funds lent (i.e., applying a "haircut" to collateral), senior creditor standing, and recourse if collateral proves insufficient. Note that the Fed has typically—but not always—imposed all of these conditions to Section 13(3) assistance. Loans to nonbanks are arguably not inherently riskier than loans to banks; to the extent that Section 13(3) programs were riskier than the discount window, it was mainly because these conditions were loosened. Lending to non-banks may also be riskier because the Fed can safeguard its lending to banks through prudential supervision, but, with the exception of firms designated as "systemically important financial institutions" (SIFIs) or structured as bank holding companies, the Fed has no jurisdiction to supervise nonbanks for safety and soundness. In times of crisis, the Fed's broader ability to restore financial stability also reduces default risk for any specific loan.

In some cases, the Fed was able to protect the taxpayer through terms other than conventional collateral pledges. For example, the Fed required that AIG provide it with compensation in the form of an equity stake in the company in exchange for a loan. The Fed's ability to protect taxpayers against losses could be more limited in the future based on a recent court ruling. The court found that the AIG equity stake was an illegal exaction.[63] However, because the Dodd-Frank Act prohibits assistance to single or failing firms, future scenarios in which the Fed would need to take an equity stake to adequately protect taxpayers may be limited.

One broader economic concern with Section 13(3) lending raised by House Financial Services Committee Chairman Jeb Hensarling is that "its use risks exacerbating moral hazard costs."[64] Moral hazard is the concept that firms will take greater risks if they are protected from negative outcomes. In this case, moral hazard occurs because firms are more likely to be more reliant on short-term lending if they anticipate access to Fed lending during a liquidity crisis. Some argue that Section 13(3) should be repealed or curbed because of moral hazard, but Bernanke compares that approach to shutting down the fire department to encourage fire safety, instead of toughening

---

[63] For more information, see CRS Legal Sidebar WSLG1300, *Court Finds AIG's Bail-Out Terms Constitute an Illegal Exaction but Awards No Damages*, by M. Maureen Murphy and David H. Carpenter (no longer distributable).

[64] Chairman Jeb Hensarling, comment letter to the Federal Reserve, docket number R-1476, January 13, 2014.

the fire code.[65] Unlike lending to banks, the Fed cannot mitigate moral hazard through prudential supervision, however, except in the cases noted above.

Moral hazard concerns can be overstated. For instance, moral hazard arguably did not cause nonbank financial firms to be reckless about liquidity management before the crisis, unless they were able to anticipate that Section 13(3) would be used to provide them with liquidity, even though it had never been used for that purpose before 2008. Thus, greater market discipline might reduce moral hazard problems but cannot eliminate liquidity crises.

How Much Discretion Should the Fed Be Granted?

Limiting discretion is the common goal running throughout many of the diverse policy proposals to alter Section 13(3). The fact that the Fed has broad discretion under Section 13(3) allowed the Fed, for or better or worse, to act swiftly, pledge sizable funds, create a diverse set of facilities for a diverse set of lenders, and tackle multiple, disparate problems as they emerged. It also explains why the Fed was able to provide assistance in forms not envisioned by Congress that arguably were not always consistent with the spirit of a lender of last resort, such as the Maiden Lane LLCs.[66]

One potential drawback to discretion is that assistance might be provided in ways the Dodd-Frank Act did not intend, such as to prevent a firm from failing. As noted above, the Dodd-Frank Act modified Section 13(3) to rule out lending to an insolvent firm, but some critics are skeptical that the Dodd-Frank Act successfully ruled out the use of Section 13(3) to aid an insolvent firm. The Fed's final rule further limits its ability to assist a failing firm by prohibiting the creation of any facility unless it is open to at least five eligible borrowers, lending to any recipient who is not current on debt over the past 90 days, lending to a healthy firm for the purposes of preventing a third party from failing (as was the case with JP Morgan Chase and Bear Stearns), and lending to a firm so that it can avoid bankruptcy or resolution. Nevertheless, as long as emergency authority exists, policymakers may be tempted to use it to bail out a failing firm to avoid a crisis—and the broader the authority, the more feasible it becomes.[67]

Arguably, another drawback to discretion is the potential for favoritism. Because the types of nonbank financial firms are numerous and diverse, deciding who should get access to loans involves trade-offs and judgments that are not completely technical in nature. For example, the Fed set a high minimum loan size in TALF that effectively limited access to loans at below-market interest rates to large investors. The decision to outsource certain functions of emergency facilities to third-party vendors also creates the potential for favoritism.[68]

---

[65] Ben Bernanke, "Warren-Vitter and the Lender of Last Resort," Brookings Institution, blog, May 15, 2015, at http://www.brookings.edu/blogs/ben-bernanke/posts/2015/05/15-warren-vitter-proposal.

[66] According to the legal counsel of the NY Fed, "The Congress that enacted Section 13(3) in the 1930's envisioned the Federal Reserve lending to companies, but it surely did not envision the Fed lending to an LLC, because that legal form of organization would not be invented for another 40 years." Thomas Baxter, "The Legal Position of the Central Bank. The Case of the Federal Reserve Bank of New York," speech delivered to *Regulatory Response to the Financial Crisis* conference, January 19, 2009.

[67] This report takes no position on whether the Fed should bail out failing firms. Bailing out firms poses tradeoffs between potential benefits to financial stability in the short run and potential costs, including moral hazard and risks to taxpayers.

[68] For details on third-party vendors, see Federal Reserve, Office of the Inspector General, *The Federal Reserve's Section 13(3) Lending Facilities to Support Overall Market Liquidity*, November 2010, p. 25 http://oig.federalreserve.gov/reports/FRS_Lending_Facilities_Report_final-11-23-10_web.pdf. The New York Fed's contracts with third-party vendors are posted at http://www.newyorkfed.org/aboutthefed/vendor_information.html.

Another consideration for the degree of discretion provided is the Fed's independence from Congress and the Administration. The Fed argues that maintaining its independence is important for the credibility and effectiveness of its monetary policy. At the same time, greater independence complicates accountability to Congress. It is fair to question to what degree limiting discretion on Section 13(3) affects perceptions of monetary policy independence because 13(3) is used so rarely. The Dodd-Frank Act's requirement that assistance under Section 13(3) be preapproved by the Treasury Secretary reduces the Fed's independence from the Administration, although the Treasury Secretary supported all of the Fed's actions taken under Section 13(3) in 2008.

Fed Chair Jerome Powell argued when he was a Fed Governor that Congress should maintain the Fed's current discretion under Section 13(3) because

> One of the lessons of the crisis is that the financial system evolves so quickly that it is difficult to predict where threats will emerge and what actions may be needed in the future to respond. Because we cannot anticipate what may be needed in the future, the Congress should preserve the ability of the Fed to respond flexibly and nimbly to future emergencies. Further restricting or eliminating the Fed's emergency lending authority will not prevent future crises, but it will hinder the Fed's ability to limit the harm from those crises for families and businesses.[69]

Alternatively, some argue that discretion can increase uncertainty, thereby increasing systemic risk. For example, some argue that the failure of Lehman Brothers exacerbated financial instability because market participants believed that it would receive Fed assistance similar to Bear Stearns and panicked when it did not.

The Dodd-Frank Act reduced the Fed's discretion under Section 13(3), and the final rule implementing those changes reduced it further. In Governor Powell's view, the Dodd-Frank reforms "struck a reasonable balance ... (and) it would be a mistake to go further and impose additional restrictions" on Section 13(3). By reducing the Fed's discretion, Chair Janet Yellen has stated that H.R. 3189 would "essentially repeal the Federal Reserve's remaining ability to act in a crisis."[70] By contrast, Chairman Hensarling believes that "Dodd-Frank tried but failed to rein in the Fed's emergency lending authority."[71]

Congress could curb discretion by adding more restrictions to Section 13(3) or by requiring Congressional approval for each action taken under Section 13(3). The latter proposal, depending on the details, could potentially affect the timeliness and credibility of the Fed's actions during a crisis. Examples of additional restrictions Congress could add to Section 13(3) include restrictions on who is eligible for assistance and the terms of assistance, such as acceptable collateral or the rate that the Fed charges (discussed below). Congress could also add limits on the amount of total assistance or assistance to one borrower.[72] Granting the Fed discretion on these issues is in part a judgment by Congress about whether it or the Fed can balance these competing

---

[69] Governor Jerome H. Powell, "'Audit the Fed' and Other Proposals," speech at the Catholic University of America, Columbus School of Law, Washington, DC, February 9, 2015, at http://www.federalreserve.gov/newsevents/speech/powell20150209a.htm.

[70] Chair Janet Yellen, *Letter to Honorable Paul Ryan and Honorable Nancy Pelosi*, November 16, 2015, at http://www.federalreserve.gov/foia/files/ryan-pelosi-letter-20151116.pdf.

[71] Chairman Jeb Hensarling, "Reining in a Sprawling Federal Reserve," *Wall Street Journal*, November 19, 2015, at http://www.wsj.com/articles/reining-in-a-sprawling-federal-reserve-1447978230?alg=y.

[72] In an earlier provision of the Dodd-Frank Act that was not enacted, total assistance under Section 13(3) would have been limited to $4 trillion.

policy considerations more effectively. For example, favoritism concerns could potentially be exacerbated or mitigated if Congress were more involved.

What Rate Should the Fed Charge?

In determining what rate the lender of last resort should charge, economists and central bankers almost universally point to the maxim of Walter Bagehot—lend freely against good collateral, but at a penalty.[73] Consensus breaks down on how penurious the penalty rate should be. A penalty rate (i.e., a rate that is higher than the market rate) achieves two goals: (1) it maximizes the return to the central bank (and thus the taxpayer) and (2) it discourages lenders from turning to the central bank instead of the private market when private credit is available (hence, the concept of lender of *last* resort), thereby reducing moral hazard problems. These two goals call for making the rate as high as possible. Alternatively, financial stability concerns call for making the rate as close to market rates as possible. Higher rates will potentially undermine financial stability by discouraging the use of Fed facilities, which may increase the stigma associated with borrowing from the Fed (i.e., if lending is made unattractive to healthy firms, the decision to borrow could be taken as a sign of desperation). Further, higher rates might weaken the health of the borrower, thereby undermining the goal of restoring stability. This concept is most starkly demonstrated in the case of assistance to AIG during the crisis (for details, see the **Appendix**). The terms of the initial Fed loan were more favorable to the taxpayer than the subsequent iterations of assistance, which were repeatedly renegotiated for fear that overly harsh terms would compromise the company's viability.

There is also a question of how a market rate should be calculated during a crisis. Generally, two features of a crisis are that markets become illiquid (so there are fewer transactions to observe) and rates become higher. These features would argue for using a pre-crisis market rate as the baseline. Critics incorrectly accused the Fed of charging below-market rates during the crisis.[74] The seeming contradiction between the low rates charged by the Fed in absolute terms and the fact that these rates were a markup above market rates is explained by the fact that the market rates referenced by the Fed were directly influenced by monetary policy. At the same time the Fed was making these loans, it was in the process of reducing the federal funds rate to zero.

The possibility of a limited group of recipients receiving below-market borrowing rates was arguably greatest in the two cases in which the direct recipients of the loans were not the intended recipients of ultimate assistance. The AMLF made loans to banks to finance the purchase of commercial paper to relieve stress in the commercial-paper market. The TALF made loans to investment funds to purchase ABS to revive the private-securitization market. Borrowers would only choose to participate in these programs if they could reasonably expect that, adjusted for risk, the profits they would earn from the purchase of commercial paper or ABS would exceed the interest on Fed loans. To entice banks and investors, respectively, to participate in these programs, the Fed made the terms of the programs relatively attractive to them (e.g., the loans were non-recourse), potentially reducing the profits and increasing the risk exposure for the Fed. Weighed against these costs, this arrangement may have had benefits to the Fed, such as avoiding the need to "pick winners" or develop the financial expertise to accurately price complex securities.

---

[73] Walter Bagehot, *Lombard Street: A Description of the Money Market* (New York: Charles Scribner's Sons, 1873).

[74] The reliability of market benchmarks is another issue. In some cases, the rate charged by the Fed was tied to LIBOR, and several banks have settled legal cases related to the manipulation of LIBOR during the financial crisis.

Section 13(3) does not address whether a penalty rate should be charged, but the final rule implementing the Dodd-Frank Act's modifications requires the Fed to charge a penalty rate, defined as a premium to the market rate prevailing in normal circumstances.

Should Borrowers' Identities Be Kept Confidential?

Many Members of Congress contend that taxpayers have a right to know to whom the Fed is lending and on what terms because taxpayers are the ultimate backstop for these loans. The Fed has argued that allowing the public to know which firms are accessing its facilities could undermine investor confidence in the institutions receiving aid because of a perception that recipients are weak or unsound. A loss of investor confidence could potentially lead to destabilizing runs on the institution's deposits, debt, or equity. If institutions feared that this would occur, the Fed argues, the institutions would be wary of participating in the Fed's programs. A delayed release of information mitigates, but does not eliminate, these concerns. Some critics would view less Fed lending as a positive outcome, but if the premise that the Fed's lender of last resort role helps prevent financial crises by maintaining the liquidity of the financial system is accepted, then an unwillingness by institutions to access Fed facilities makes the system less safe. One study argues that the Fed's decision to discourage banks to use the discount window from 1929-1931 (at a time when identities were kept confidential) worsened the bank panic in the Great Depression.[75]

Whether investors are less willing to borrow as a result of the disclosure of identities will not be apparent until the next crisis. A historical example supporting the Fed's argument would be the experience with the Reconstruction Finance Corporation (RFC) in the Great Depression. When the RFC publicized to which banks it had given loans, those banks typically experienced depositor runs.[76] A more recent example—disclosure of TARP fund recipients—provides mixed evidence. At first, TARP funds were widely disbursed, and recipients included all the major banks. At that point, there was no perceived stigma to TARP participation. Subsequently, many banks repaid TARP shares at the first opportunity, and several remaining participants have expressed concern that if they did not repay soon, investors would perceive them as weak.

The granularity of information to be disclosed is a policy issue. Aggregate information about programs and activities that does not require the identification of borrowers tends to be more useful for broad policy purposes, while current information on specific transactions within the programs is of interest to investors. The Fed voluntarily released the former, but only reluctantly released the latter when compelled to by legislation and lawsuits. For oversight purposes, the former would suffice for answering most questions about taxpayer risk exposure, expected profits or losses, potential subsidies, economic effects, and evaluating the state of the financial system. The latter would be necessary for transparency around issues such as favoritism (certain firms receiving preferential treatment over similar firms).[77] Although preventing favoritism is a valid policy goal, releasing the identities of borrowers to "name and shame" them is more questionable, especially if one believes that these programs were helpful for providing liquidity and maintaining financial stability. Naming and shaming is likely to result in less uptake of the programs in the future. If one believes that these lending programs are not helpful, repealing

---

[75] Gary Gorton and Andrew Metrick, "The Federal Reserve and Panic Prevention," *Journal of Economic Perspectives*, vol. 27, no. 4, Fall 2013, p. 53.

[76] James Butkiewicz, "The Reconstruction Finance Corporation, the Gold Standard, and the Banking Panic of 1933," *Southern Economic Journal*, vol. 66, no. 2, October 1999, p. 271.

[77] Another option for addressing these types of questions would be to allow GAO, the Fed's Inspector General, or some other outside group to investigate confidential material without releasing it to the public.

Section 13(3) would be more effective than undermining their effectiveness by stigmatizing recipients.

As discussed above, the Dodd-Frank Act compromised between stability and oversight concerns by requiring borrowers' identities to be publicly released with a lag. Some Members of Congress have expressed an interest in revisiting this issue.

Selected Legislation

114th Congress

One bill to amend Section 13(3) (H.R. 3189) passed the House in the 114th Congress. Other bills to amend Section 13(3) that did not see legislative action were H.R. 5983, S. 1320, and H.R. 2625.

H.R. 3189

The Fed Oversight Reform and Modernization Act (H.R. 3189) was ordered to be reported by the House Financial Services Committee on July 29, 2015. On November 19, 2015, it was passed by the House. Section 11 of the bill as passed amends Section 13(3) to limit the Fed's discretion to make emergency loans. It would limit 13(3) to "unusual and exigent circumstances that pose a threat to the financial stability of the United States" and would require "the affirmative vote of not less than nine presidents of Federal reserve banks" in addition to the current requirement of the affirmative vote of five Fed governors. It would forbid the Fed from accepting as collateral equity securities issued by a borrower. It would require the Fed to issue a rule establishing how it would determine sufficiency of collateral; acceptable classes of collateral; any discount that would be applied to determine the sufficiency of collateral; and how it would obtain independent appraisals for valuing collateral. It would eliminate the current language permitting the Fed to establish the solvency of a borrower based on the borrower's certification and would specify that before a borrower may be eligible for assistance, the Fed's Board and any other federal banking regulator with jurisdiction over the borrower must certify that the borrower is not insolvent. It would limit assistance to institutions "predominantly engaged in financial activities" and preclude assistance to federal, state, and local government agencies and government-controlled or sponsored entities. It would require the Fed to issue a rule establishing a minimum interest rate on emergency loans based on the sum of the average secondary discount rate charged by the Federal Reserve banks over the most recent 90-day period and the average of the difference between a distressed corporate bond index (as defined by a rule issued by the Fed) and the Treasury yield over the most recent 90-day period.

H.R. 5983

The same language amending 13(3) from H.R. 3189 was then included in the Financial Choice Act of 2016 (H.R. 5983), a wide-ranging financial regulatory relief bill sponsored by Jeb Hensarling, Chairman of the Financial Services Committee.[78] H.R. 5983 was ordered to be reported as amended by the House Committee on Financial Services on September 13, 2016, and was reported on December 20, 2016.

---

[78] For more information, see CRS Report R44631, *The Financial CHOICE Act in the 114th Congress: Policy Issues*, coordinated by Sean M. Hoskins.

115th Congress

One bill to amend Section 13(3) (H.R. 10) passed the House in the 115th Congress. Other bills to amend Section 13(3) that were reported by the House Financial Services Committee were H.R. 4302 and H.R. 6741.

H.R. 10

The same language amending 13(3) from H.R. 3189 in the 114th Congress was included in the Financial Choice Act of 2017 (H.R. 10), a wide-ranging financial regulatory relief bill sponsored by Jeb Hensarling, Chairman of the Financial Services Committee.[79] H.R. 10 was passed by the House on June 8, 2017.

---

[79] For more information, see CRS Report R44839, *The Financial CHOICE Act in the 115th Congress: Selected Policy Issues*, by Marc Labonte et al.

Appendix. Details on the Actions Taken Under Section 13(3) in 2008

Term Securities Lending Facility

Shortly before Bear Stearns suffered its liquidity crisis, the Fed created the Term Securities Lending Facility (TSLF) on March 11, 2008, to expand its existing securities lending program for primary dealers.[80] Primary dealers are financial firms that are the Fed's counterparties for open market operations, including investment banks that were ineligible to access the Fed's lending facilities for banks. At the end of 2007, there were 20 primary dealers, including Bear Stearns.[81] The proximate cause of Bear Stearns' crisis was its inability to roll over its short-term debt, and the Fed created the TSLF and the Primary Dealer Credit Facility (discussed below) to offer an alternative source of short-term liquidity for primary dealers.

Primary dealers were already allowed to borrow securities from the Fed on an overnight basis before the crisis. The TSLF extended the length of the loans and acceptable collateral, and signaled that the Fed was willing to lend on a larger scale. Under the TSLF at its peak, each week primary dealers could borrow up to $200 billion of Treasury securities for 28 days, as opposed to overnight. Primary dealers need access to Treasury securities because of their use in repurchase agreements (repos), which are an important source of short-term financing. **Figure A-1** shows the decline in primary dealer repos outstanding in 2008. At various points, loans could be collateralized with some of the following: private-label mortgage-backed securities (MBS) with an AAA/Aaa rating, agency commercial MBS, agency collateralized mortgage obligations, and all investment-grade debt securities. On July 30, 2008, the Fed created the TSLF Options Program within the TSLF that allowed primary dealers to pre-negotiate options to borrow securities. No securities were borrowed through the TSLF after August 2009, and the facility expired February 1, 2010. The TSLF experienced no losses and earned income of $781 million over the life of the program.

---

[80] For more information, see New York Fed documents collection on the TSLF posted at http://www.newyorkfed.org/markets/tslf.html.

[81] The official list of current primary dealers is posted at http://www.newyorkfed.org/markets/pridealers_current.html. Lists of past primary dealers are available at http://www.newyorkfed.org/markets/Dealer_Lists_1960_to_2014.xls.

Figure A-1. Primary Dealer Repos Outstanding

(2002-2012, weekly)

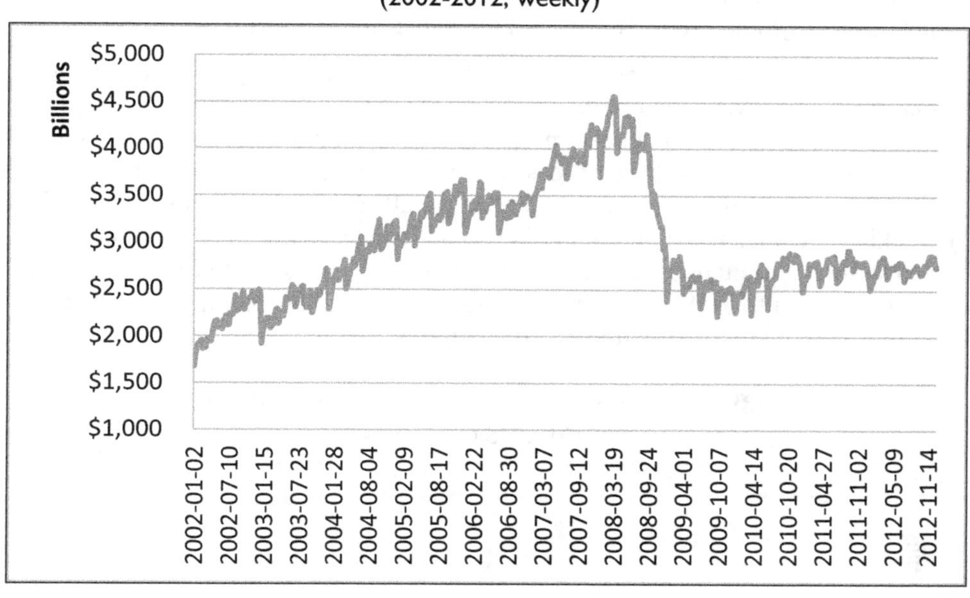

Source: New York Fed, Primary Dealer Statistics.

Note: Includes overnight, continuing, and term agreement repos.

Primary Dealer Credit Facility

Shortly after Bear Stearns' liquidity crisis, the Fed created the Primary Dealer Credit Facility (PDCF) on March 16, 2008. The PDCF can be thought of as analogous to a discount window for primary dealers.[82] Loans were made at the Fed's discount rate, which was set slightly higher than the federal funds rate during the crisis. Loans were made on an overnight basis, with recourse, and they were fully collateralized, limiting their riskiness. Acceptable collateral at times included Treasuries; government agency debt; investment grade corporate, mortgage-backed, asset-backed, and municipal securities; and certain classes of equities. The PDCF expired on February 1, 2010.

Borrowing from the facility was sporadic, with average daily borrowing outstanding above $10 billion in the first three months and falling to zero in August 2008. Much of this initial borrowing was done by Bear Stearns, before its merger with JPMorgan Chase was complete. Borrowing picked up again in September 2008 and peaked at $148 billion on October 1, 2008. No loans were outstanding after May 2009. The PDCF experienced no losses and earned interest income of $0.5 billion over the life of the program.

Commercial Paper Funding Facility and Asset-Backed Commercial Paper Money Market Mutual Fund Liquidity Facility

To meet liquidity needs, many large firms routinely issue commercial paper, which is short-term debt purchased directly by investors that matures in less than 270 days, with an average maturity of 30 days. The three broad categories of commercial paper issuers are financial firms,

---

[82] For more information, see New York Fed documents collection on the PDCF posted at http://www.newyorkfed.org/markets/pdcf.html; Tobias Adrian et al., *The Federal Reserve's Primary Dealer Credit Facility*, Current Issues in Economics and Finance, vol. 15, no. 4, August 2009, at http://www.newyorkfed.org/research/current_issues/ci15-4.pdf.

nonfinancial firms, and pass-through entities that issue commercial paper backed by assets. The commercial paper issued directly by firms tends not to be backed by collateral, because these firms are viewed as large and creditworthy, and the paper matures quickly.

Individual investors are major purchasers of highly rated commercial paper through money market mutual funds (MMMFs) and money market accounts. On September 16, 2008, a MMMF called the Reserve Fund "broke the buck," meaning that the value of its shares had fallen below par value of $1. This occurred because of losses it had taken on short-term debt issued by Lehman Brothers, which filed for bankruptcy on September 15, 2008. Money market investors had perceived breaking the buck to be highly unlikely, and its occurrence set off a generalized run on MMMFs, as investors simultaneously attempted to withdraw an estimated $250 billion of their investments—even from funds without exposure to Lehman.[83] The decline in commercial paper outstanding after September 2008 is illustrated in **Figure A-2**.

Figure A-2. Commercial Paper Outstanding

(2000:Q1-2015:Q1, quarterly)

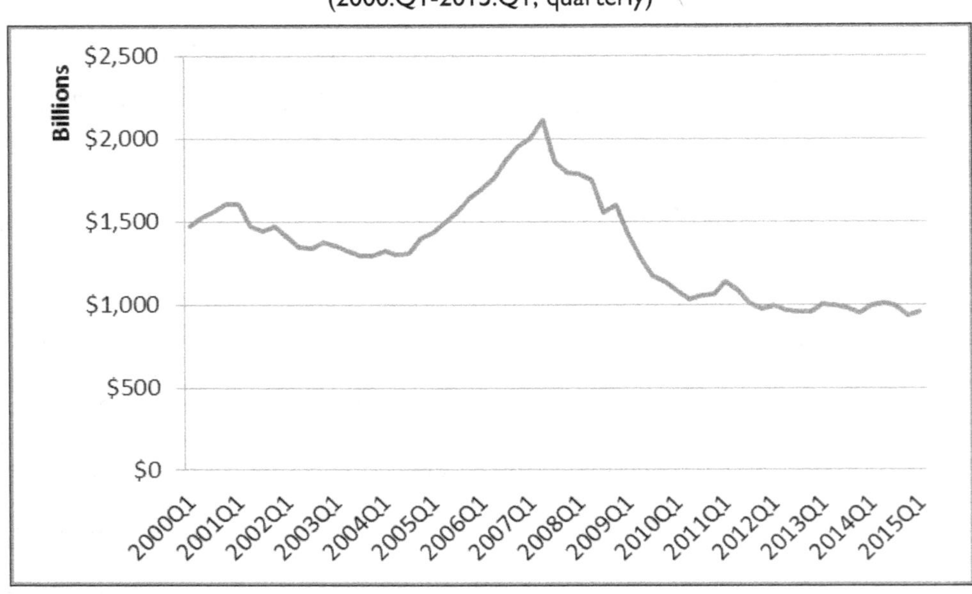

Source: Federal Reserve, Z.1 release.

Fearing that disruption in the commercial paper markets could make overall problems in financial markets more severe, the Fed announced on September 19, 2008, that it would create the Asset-Backed Commercial Paper Money Market Mutual Fund Liquidity Facility (AMLF). This facility made nonrecourse loans to banks to purchase asset-backed commercial paper. As the commercial paper matured, the loans were repaid. Because the loans were nonrecourse, the banks had no further liability to repay any losses on the commercial paper collateralizing the loan. At its peak in early October 2008, the AMLF had loans of $152 billion outstanding. However, the AMLF would soon be superseded in importance by the creation of the Commercial Paper Funding Facility (CPFF), and lending fell to zero in October 2009. The AMLF experienced no losses and

---

[83] Figure cited in Fed Chairman Ben Bernanke, "Financial Reform to Address Systemic Risk," speech at the Council on Foreign Relations, March 10, 2009, at http://www.federalreserve.gov/newsevents/speech/bernanke20090310a.htm.

earned income of $0.5 billion over the life of the program. The facility expired on February 1, 2010.

On October 7, 2008, the Fed announced the creation of the CPFF to purchase all types of three-month, highly rated U.S. commercial paper, secured and unsecured, from issuers.[84] The CPFF charged an interest rate equal to the three-month overnight index swap rate plus 1 percentage point for secured corporate debt, 2 percentage points for unsecured corporate debt, and 3 percentage points for asset-backed paper. The CPFF could buy as much commercial paper from any individual issuer as that issuer had outstanding in the year to date. Any potential losses borne by the CPFF would ultimately be borne by the Fed. At its peak in January 2009, the CPFF held $351 billion of commercial paper, and holdings fell steadily subsequently. The facility expired February 1, 2010. It earned income of $6.1 billion over the life of the program and suffered no losses.

In the case of the AMLF, the banks were not intended recipients of assistance, but rather were the intermediary through which assistance flowed to the commercial paper market. According to GAO, 92% of credit extended under AMLF was channeled through two custodial banks (JPMorgan Chase and State Street) that were among the three largest providers of fund administration and account services for MMMFs.[85] The CPFF removed the role of banks as intermediary and provided Fed assistance directly to commercial paper issuers.[86]

On October 21, 2008, the Fed announced the creation of the Money Market Investor Funding Facility (MMIFF) and pledged to lend it up to $540 billion. The MMIFF was planned to lend to private-sector special purpose vehicles (SPVs) that invest in commercial paper issued by highly rated financial institutions. Each SPV would have been owned by a group of financial firms and could only purchase commercial paper issued by that group. The intent was for these SPVs to purchase commercial paper from money market mutual funds and similar entities facing redemption requests to help avoid runs, such as the run on the Reserve Fund. The MMIFF was never accessed, and the facility expired on October 30, 2009.

Term Asset-Backed Securities Loan Facility

On November 25, 2008, the Fed created the Term Asset-Backed Securities Loan Facility (TALF) in response to problems in the market for asset-backed securities (ABS).[87] According to the Fed, "new issuance of ABS declined precipitously in September and came to a halt in October. At the same time, interest rate spreads on AAA-rated tranches of ABS soared to levels well outside the

---

[84] For more information, see New York Fed documents collection on the CPFF posted at http://www.newyorkfed.org/markets/cpff.html; Tobias Adrian et al., "The Federal Reserve's Commercial Paper Funding Facility," Federal Reserve Bank of New York, *Economic Policy Review*, May 2011, p. 25, at http://www.newyorkfed.org/research/epr/11v17n1/1105adri.pdf.

[85] U.S. Government Accountability Office (GAO), *Federal Reserve System: Opportunities Exist to Strengthen Policies and Processes for Managing Emergency Assistance*, GAO-11-696, July 21, 2011, Table 12, at http://www.gao.gov/new.items/d11696.pdf.

[86] To comply with statute, the CPFF was set up as a special purpose vehicle (SPV) controlled by the Fed that borrowed from the Fed to finance its commercial paper purchases.

[87] For more information, see New York Fed documents collection on TALF posted at http://www.newyorkfed.org/markets/talf.html and http://www.newyorkfed.org/research/epr/12v18n3/1210ashc.pdf; Sumit Agarwal, Jacqueline Barrett, Crystal Cun, and Mariacristina De Nardi, "The asset-backed securities markets, the crisis, and TALF," Federal Reserve Bank of Chicago, *Economic Perspectives*, 4Q/2010, p. 101, at https://www.chicagofed.org/~/media/publications/economic-perspectives/2010/4qtr2010-part1-agarwal-barrett-cun-denardi-pdf.pdf.

---

range of historical experience, reflecting unusually high risk premiums."[88] The decline in ABS issuance is illustrated in **Figure A-3**. The Fed feared that if lenders could not securitize these types of loans, less credit would be extended to consumers, exacerbating the economic downturn.

Figure A-3. Asset-Backed Securities Issuance

(2000-2015, annually)

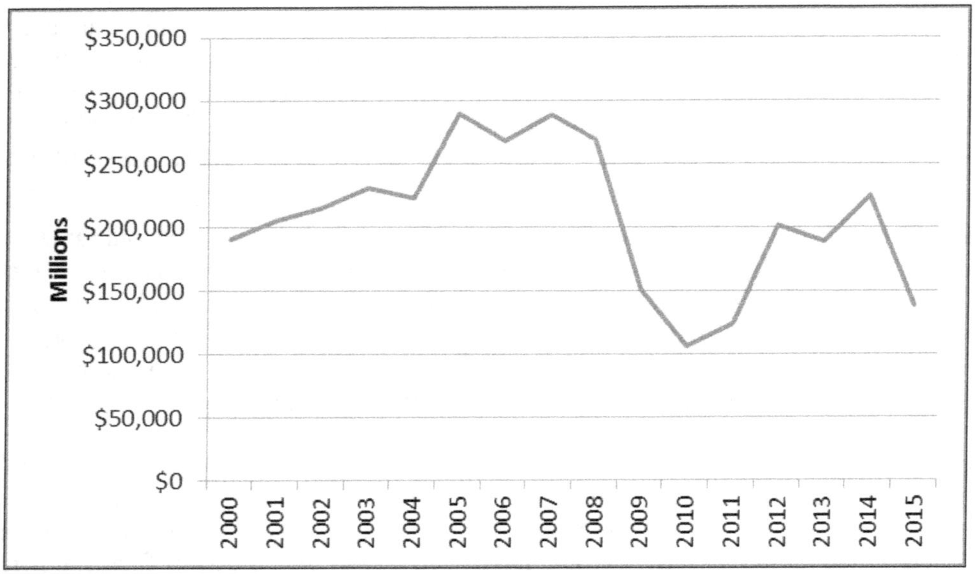

Source: Securities Industry and Financial Markets Association, data accessed at http://www.sifma.org/ uploadedFiles/Research/Statistics/StatisticsFiles/SF-US-ABS-SIFMA.xls?n=55152.

Note: Does not include mortgage-backed securities.

Rather than purchase ABS directly, the Fed made nonrecourse loans to private investment funds to purchase recently issued ABS with the highest credit rating, using the ABS as collateral. The minimum loan size was $10 million. Eligible collateral included new securities backed by auto loans, student loans, small business loans, and credit card loans. TALF was later expanded to include "legacy" commercial MBS. The loans had a term of up to three years for most types of assets (and up to five years for some types of assets), but were repaid when the underlying ABS matured or was sold. Interest rates were set at a markup over different maturities of the London Interbank Offered Rate (LIBOR) or the federal funds rate, depending on the type of loan and underlying collateral.

If the ABS had lost value, because the loans were nonrecourse, the losses would have been borne by the Fed and the Treasury (through TARP) instead of by the borrower—an unusual feature that made TALF riskier for taxpayers than typical Fed lending facilities. The Fed lent less than the market value of the collateral, so the Fed would not have borne losses on the loans until losses exceeded the value of this "haircut" (different ABS receive different haircuts). In addition, Treasury initially set aside $20 billion of TARP funds to cover any losses.[89]

Peaking at $48 billion, TALF turned out to be a relatively small program compared with the $200 billion program envisioned by the Fed or the $1 trillion program later envisioned by Treasury. In

---

[88] Federal Reserve, "Federal Reserve Announces the Creation of the Term Asset-Backed Securities Loan Facility (TALF)," press release, November 25, 2008.

[89] On July 20, 2010, Treasury reduced its loss exposure to $4.3 billion, maintaining the 10% maximum loss exposure in light of the actual loans outstanding when the program ended.

part, this was because the issuance of assets eligible for TALF remained low, which reflected the depressed state of securitization markets and may imply that TALF was unable to overcome investor aversion to ABS. (While TALF was in operation beginning in March 2009, a sizable share of ABS issued were used as collateral for TALF loans. Thus, issuance might have been even lower without the presence of TALF.)

Unlike most other Fed lending facilities, the amount outstanding under TALF steadily rose through 2009. The facility stopped making new loans at the end of June 2010 for loans using newly issued commercial MBS as collateral and in March 2010 for loans using other assets. The last TALF loan was repaid on October 29, 2014. All TALF loans were repaid in full, with interest.[90] Over the life of the program, TALF made profits of $1.6 billion for the Fed and $0.7 billion for the Treasury.

Bear Stearns

Unable to roll over its short-term debt as a result of investor concerns about its mortgage-related losses, the investment bank Bear Stearns faced bankruptcy in 2008. Fearing that Bear Stearns was "too big to fail" and posed systemic risk,[91] the Fed stepped in to broker a merger. On March 14, 2008, the Fed provided a $12.9 billion bridge loan on a nonrecourse basis to JP Morgan Chase to provide Bear Stearns with liquidity, which was repaid with interest. On March 16, JPMorgan Chase agreed to acquire Bear Stearns. As part of the agreement, the Fed agreed to lend $28.82 billion to Maiden Lane I, a Delaware limited liability corporation (LLC) that it created, to purchase financial securities at market value from Bear Stearns. These securities were largely mortgage-related assets that were too illiquid for JPMorgan Chase to be willing to acquire.

Maiden Lane I, not JP Morgan Chase, was to repay the Fed interest and principal using the funds from the sale of the assets. JP Morgan Chase took a first loss position through a subordinated loan of $1.15 billion, receiving an interest rate of 4.5% above the discount rate on that position, compared with an interest rate of 2.5% above the discount rate on the Fed's loan. Any additional losses would be borne by the Fed, and any profits in excess of the loans would accrue to the Fed. Profits or losses for the Fed and JP Morgan Chase were dependent on whether the market value of those assets rose or declined after Maiden Lane I acquired them.

By November 2012, proceeds from the sale or maturation of Maiden Lane I assets were sufficient to fully repay principal and accrued interest to the Fed ($765 million) and JP Morgan Chase. As of December 30, 2014, the value of remaining assets held by Maiden Lane I was $1.7 billion.[92] Once those remaining assets are sold or have matured, the Fed will realize additional capital gains that would be greater or less than $1.7 billion (less expenses), depending on whether the value of those assets subsequently rises or falls.

---

[90] Federal Reserve, *Final Report Pursuant to Section 129(b)*, November 21, 2014, at http://www.federalreserve.gov/monetarypolicy/files/129periodicupdate20141121.pdf.

[91] For more information, see CRS Report R42150, *Systemically Important or "Too Big to Fail" Financial Institutions*, by Marc Labonte.

[92] Federal Reserve Bank of New York, *Maiden Lane Transactions*, at http://www.newyorkfed.org/markets/maidenlane.html.

American International Group

In September 2008, facing losses on various operations, AIG experienced a significant decline in its stock price and downgrades from the major credit rating agencies.[93] These downgrades led to immediate demands for significant amounts of collateral (approximately $14 billion to $15 billion in collateral payments, according to contemporary press reports).[94] As financial demands on the company mounted, bankruptcy appeared a possibility, as had occurred with Lehman Brothers on September 15, 2008. Many feared that AIG was too big to fail due to the potential for widespread disruption to financial markets resulting from such a failure.

On September 16, 2008 (prior to the existence of TARP), the Fed announced that it was taking action to support AIG in the form of a secured two-year line of credit with a value of up to $85 billion and an interest rate of 8.5 percentage points above the three-month LIBOR. In addition, the government received warrants to purchase up to 79.9% of the equity in AIG. On October 8, 2008, the Fed announced that it would lend AIG up to an additional $37.8 billion against securities held by its insurance subsidiaries.[95]

In early November 2008 (following the creation of TARP), the financial support for AIG was restructured. The restructured financial support consisted of (1) reducing the size of the Fed loan to up to $60 billion, with the term lengthened to five years and the interest rate reduced by 5.5 percentage points; (2) purchasing $40 billion in preferred shares through TARP; and (3) replacing the $37.8 billion loan with up to $52.5 billion total in asset purchases by the Fed through two LLCs known as Maiden Lane II and Maiden Lane III. The 79.9% equity position of the government in AIG remained essentially unchanged after the restructuring of the intervention.

In March 2009, the assistance was restructured further through (1) a partial payback of the Fed loan through a swap of debt for equity in two AIG subsidiaries worth approximately $25 billion, reducing the maximum to $35 billion and (2) commitments for additional future TARP purchases of up to $29.8 billion in preferred shares at AIG's discretion, and the conversion of existing shares into shares with optional dividend payments.[96] The Maiden Lane LLCs continued operating under the previous terms, with the actual loans extended to the LLCs totaling $43.9 billion at their peak.

In September 2010, AIG and the government announced another restructuring of the government's assistance. This restructuring closed on January 14, 2011. The expressed goal was to simplify the government's interest in AIG and provide a path for the government to divest its stake in AIG. The essence of the plan called for (1) ending the Fed's involvement with AIG through loan repayment and transfer of the Fed's equity interests to Treasury and (2) converting the government's $49.1 billion in existing preferred shares into common shares, which could then be sold to the public over time. The specific steps involved several interlocking transactions,

---

[93] For details on the Fed's assistance, see New York Fed, *Actions Related to AIG*, at http://www.newyorkfed.org/aboutthefed/aig/index.html. For more information on the federal assistance to AIG, see CRS Report R42953, *Government Assistance for AIG: Summary and Cost*, by Baird Webel.

[94] See, for example, "U.S. to Take Over AIG in $85 Billion Bailout; Central Banks Inject Cash as Credit Dries Up," *Wall Street Journal*, September 17, 2008, pp. A1-A6.

[95] In October 2008, AIG also announced that it had applied to the Fed's broadly available Commercial Paper Funding Facility (CPFF) and was approved to borrow up to $20.9 billion at the facility's standard terms. At its peak use in January 2009, AIG had commercial paper worth $16.1 billion outstanding from the CPFF. AIG continued to access the facility until it expired in February 2010. Over the life of the facility, AIG paid $0.4 billion in interest to the CPFF. AIG's use of the CPFF is included in the CPFF totals, not the AIG totals, in this report.

[96] AIG issued $1.6 billion of additional preferred shares to the government in recognition of accrued, unpaid dividends on the initial $40 billion in assistance.

---

including the initial public offering of a large AIG subsidiary, the sale of several other AIG subsidiaries, and the use of up to approximately $20 billion in TARP funds to transfer equity interests from the Fed to the Treasury.

All of the Fed loans have been repaid, and the assets held in the Maiden Lane LLCs have been sold. Maiden Lanes II and III were formally terminated on November 12, 2014. The Fed earned interest of $8.2 billion on the loan to AIG and $9.5 billion on the Maiden Lanes. In addition to the income received by the Fed, Treasury received an additional $17.6 billion on the sale of equity that the Fed originally received (and subsequently transferred to the Treasury) as recompense for the Fed's loan to AIG.

Citigroup

On November, 23, 2008, the Treasury, Fed, and Federal Deposit Insurance Corporation (FDIC) announced a joint intervention in Citigroup, which had previously received $25 billion in TARP Capital Purchase Program funding.[97] This exceptional intervention to "[support] financial stability" consisted of an additional $20 billion purchase of preferred shares through the TARP Targeted Investment Program and a government guarantee for a pool of $306 billion in Citigroup assets (reduced to $301 billion when the guarantee was finalized on January 16, 2009) through the TARP Asset Guarantee Program, the FDIC, and the Fed.[98]

In December 2009, Citigroup and Treasury reached an agreement to cancel the asset guarantee. While the asset guarantee was in place, no losses were claimed and no federal funds were paid out. The Fed's share of the termination fee for the asset guarantee was $50 million.[99]

Bank of America

On January 16, 2009, the Treasury, Fed, and FDIC announced a joint intervention in Bank of America, which had previously received $25 billion in TARP Capital Purchase Program funds. Bank of America's losses were largest at Merrill Lynch, which it was in the process of taking over. The Fed and Treasury may have been most concerned that if Bank of America was not offered special assistance, the merger would fall through and Merrill Lynch would experience a disorderly failure. "[A]s part of its commitment to support financial market stability,"[100] this exceptional assistance included the purchase of an additional $20 billion of Bank of America preferred shares through the TARP Targeted Investment Program and a joint guarantee on a pool of up to $118 billion of certain Bank of America assets (largely those acquired through its merger with Merrill Lynch). The announced guarantee was to remain in place for 10 years for residential mortgage-related assets and 5 years for all other assets. Bank of America would have borne up to

---

[97] U.S. Treasury, "Joint Statement by Treasury, Federal Reserve, and FDIC on Citigroup," press release hp-1287, November 23, 2008.

[98] For information on Citigroup's TARP shares, see CRS Report R41427, *Troubled Asset Relief Program (TARP): Implementation and Status*, by Baird Webel.

[99] U.S. Treasury, "Treasury Prices Sale of Citigroup Subordinated Notes for Proceeds of $894 Million, Providing an Additional Profit for Taxpayers on TARP Citigroup Investment," press release, February 5, 2013, at http://www.treasury.gov/press-center/press-releases/Pages/tg1841.aspx; U.S. Treasury, "Taxpayers Receive $10.5 Billion In Proceeds Today From Final Sale Of Treasury Department Citigroup Common Stock," press release, December 10, 2010, at http://www.financialstability.gov/latest/pr_12102010.html; Federal Reserve, "Support for Specific Institutions," available at http://www.federalreserve.gov/monetarypolicy/bst_supportspecific.htm.

[100] U.S. Treasury, "Treasury, Federal Reserve, and the FDIC Provide Assistance to Bank of America," press release hp1356, January 16, 2009.

---

the first $10 billion of losses on the assets, with subsequent losses split 90% to the government and 10% to Bank of America. Within the government, the losses were to be split between the TARP Asset Guarantee Program, the FDIC, and the Fed.

Although the asset guarantee was announced in January 2009, a final agreement was never signed. On September 21, 2009, Bank of America announced that it had negotiated a $425 million termination fee (of which, the Fed received $57 million) that allowed it to withdraw from the Asset Guarantee Program.[101]

Author Information

Marc Labonte
Specialist in Macroeconomic Policy

Acknowledgments

The **Appendix** is adapted from CRS Report R43413, *Costs of Government Interventions in Response to the Financial Crisis: A Retrospective*, by Baird Webel and Marc Labonte. "Selected Legislation in the 114th Congress" and "The Fed's Rule Implementing the Dodd-Frank Act's Changes" were co-authored with M. Maureen Murphy, legislative attorney.

Disclaimer

This document was prepared by the Congressional Research Service (CRS). CRS serves as nonpartisan shared staff to congressional committees and Members of Congress. It operates solely at the behest of and under the direction of Congress. Information in a CRS Report should not be relied upon for purposes other than public understanding of information that has been provided by CRS to Members of Congress in connection with CRS's institutional role. CRS Reports, as a work of the United States Government, are not subject to copyright protection in the United States. Any CRS Report may be reproduced and distributed in its entirety without permission from CRS. However, as a CRS Report may include copyrighted images or material from a third party, you may need to obtain the permission of the copyright holder if you wish to copy or otherwise use copyrighted material.

---

[101] U.S. Treasury, "Asset Guarantee Program," available at http://www.treasury.gov/initiatives/financial-stability/ TARP-Programs/bank-investment-programs/agp/Pages/overview.aspx. The termination agreement is available at http://www.treasury.gov/initiatives/financial-stability/programs/investment-programs/agp/Documents/BofA%20- %20Termination%20Agreement%20-%20executed.pdf.